Your Chromebook

The Essential Guide to Cloud Computing with the Google Pixelbook and other Chromebooks

Tony Loton

www.yourchromebook.com

Published by LOTONtech Limited, www.lotontech.com.

Print ISBN-13: 978-1978195417

Print ISBN-10: 1978195419

Contents

About the Book

I've been on quite a journey since I wrote the first book about the chromebook way back in 2011. In sympathy with the quickly-evolving chromebook concept, I published the first four editions of "The Chrome Book" in relatively rapid succession. Then I slowed down somewhat as the cloud computing and chromebook markets began to mature. I wrote the fifth edition of the original book about eighteen months after publishing the fourth edition, and it's now been nearly three years since I last tackled this topic. The end result is this new book:

Your Chrome Book: The Essential Guide to Cloud Computing with the Google Pixelbook and other Chromebooks

Along my journey I have seen several different chromebook incarnations, and have almost always used the latest and greatest chromebook as the test vehicle for each retelling of the story: from the original very-affordable ARM-powered Samsung chromebook to the outrageously overpriced and (then) top-of-the-range Chromebook Pixel. The only exception was the fifth edition of the book, in which I widened the scope to include more information about using Google's cloud computing services without a chromebook: on Android smartphones and tablets (via dedicated Android apps and the Chrome web browser) and on a traditional PC running the Chrome web browser in Windows 8 mode. Not only did this allow readers to try Google's interpretation of cloud computing before even buying a chromebook; it also emphasized the ethos that cloud computing is all about accessing your cloud-based services and storage from anywhere in the world using any compatible device – chromebook, Android tablet, or Windows PC – as long as it runs the Chrome web browser.

Whatever chromebook model or other device you're using, you should find that this book has something to say. While different devices and models of device may have faster processors, more memory, a better keyboard, or a more competitive price, they will all operate in much the same way when it comes to cloud computing via the Chrome web browser.

As you join me on the latest leg of my chromebook journey, you will find that I have once again focused on one particular chromebook model: the Google Pixelbook. But you don't have to own or aspire to own a Pixelbook in order to make the most of this book.

I've made some other changes too in response to constructive criticism from reviewers of the previous books:

- I've concentrated more on chromebooks and the Chrome OS in the earlier chapters, so that you can get up-and-running with your new device without unnecessary delay.
- I've saved my wider coverage of cloud computing concepts for the later chapters, for the benefit those of you who want to know more about what computing in the cloud really means for a regular Joe or Josephine.
- I've simplified some of the language so that this book reads rather less like it was written by a computer science graduate.

While it's taken some time for chromebooks to really take hold, I am pleased to report that Google's persistence with its once-experimental attempt to provide a non-Windows personal computer seems to be paying off. Increasing numbers of people are now purchasing chromebooks instead of traditional PCs, particularly (but not only) in environments such as education.

About the Author

I published the previous editions of this book (then titled "The Chrome Book") under the pseudonym C H Rome, for no other reason than I thought it was funny for the name of this pseudo-author to spell out the word 'Chrome'. It wasn't quite so funny when one or two reviewers of the original book(s) on Amazon tried to 'out' me because they thought I was deliberately distancing myself from my work. So now I'm outing myself:

Tony Loton is "creative director" of his one-man-band publishing company. When not contracted to write for commercial clients, he works with words and pictures as a freelance writer, editor, publishing consultant and sometimes journalist.

www.lotontech.com

Introduction to Chromebooks and Cloud Computing

This book is all about Cloud Computing with chromebooks, so in this introductory chapter I will briefly set out what a chromebook is, what cloud computing is, and how the two concepts come together.

*Just bought a Google Pixelbook, or thinking about buying one? Feel free to skip ahead to the chapter titled **A Pixelbook Primer**.*

*Just bought another kind of chromebook, and you really don't care (right now now) about the background to chromebooks and cloud computing? Feel free to skip ahead to the **Chromebook Installation and Initialization*** chapter.

About Chromebooks

A chromebook is a new kind of computer, or it at least it was some six or so years ago when Google conceived the concept of a fast-booting, low-power, low-maintenance, high-security, easy-to-use, always-connected device:

➢ **Fast-booting:** Personal computers were traditionally slow to start up, so Google conceived a computer that could get up to speed rapidly from a standing start, not only when coming out of standby mode by lifting the lid or pressing the power button.

➢ **Low-power:** With fewer "moving parts" such as fans and spinning disk drives, chromebooks can typically go a long time between charges.

➢ **Low-maintenance:** Mere mortals really don't want to be bothered with making sure their device drivers (e.g. for printers) are up-to-date, so Google wanted to do away with user-installed device drivers and programs.

➢ **High-security:** With little or no self-installed software, there would be little-to-no prospect of malicious apps causing mayhem on chromebooks by introducing computer viruses. And no viruses would mean no need for anti-virus software.

➢ **Easy-to-use:** You know how to use a web browser, right? And how to take advantage of Android apps on your mobile phone? In which case, you're well on the way to becoming a chromebook connoisseur... with a little help from this book, of course.

➢ **Always-connected:** Just as you don't expect to connect your smartphone explicitly to the internet, with a chromebook you are (almost) always connected, except when you want to work on a document or watch a movie in a no-signal zone.

Who Would Want a Chromebook?

Some stereotypical people who may prefer to use a chromebook rather than a traditional Windows PC (or similar) are:

- **Tina** is a student living away from home. She likes to socialize via Facebook, to email the folks back home, and to write the occasional essay for her classes via the university-provided free Wi-Fi.
- **Tim** wants to get his elderly parents online without the burden of resolving software installation issues and keeping antivirus software up to date. He merely wants to provide them with a "window on the web" and a proper keyboard rather than only a tablet touchscreen.
- **Terry** is a freelance journalist who researches topics and submits articles to magazine editors, and who otherwise spends his time reading the news and managing his money online.
- **Tracy** runs a real estate office. Her employees need to take pictures of properties and write descriptions while out in the field, and publish these to the web before even returning to the office. Tracy has a very limited budget for IT support, so a set of team chromebooks (with companion Android smartphones) backed by the business-oriented Google Apps may be suitable for her and her staff.

Who Wouldn't Want a Chromebook?

Chromebooks may not be for everyone, and some obvious (to me) exceptions include:

- **Toby** is a trendy "man about town" who puts style before substance and who likes to show off his cool-brand gadgets to his friends, even though he doesn't use those gadgets to even half their potential. He may well be an Apple aficionado, and the cheaper chromebooks are probably not for him... although the Google Pixelbook may well be!
- **Trisha** is a computer games developer who writes code using a special PC-based software development kit. Her media-rich creations necessitate the use of a top-of-the-range video and audio editing software suite. The chromebook is probably not for her. But when not developing computer games, she can still practice cloud computing by using the Chrome web browser and the companion Google Drive program on her Windows PC.

Not so long ago I would have included "creatives" such as artists and graphic designers in my list of people who would prefer a different kind of computer such as a Macbook or Microsoft Surface. Well, the Google Pixelbook has changed all that with its variable form factors, tablet touchscreen, Pixelbook Pen and support for Android apps.

About Cloud Computing

Cloud computing is all about ditching the hard drive except for the temporary storage of documents you're currently writing or the movies you're currently watching. It's about not losing your life's work when your computer crashes or you suffer a hard disk disaster. It's about accessing your files from any compatible device anywhere in the world. It's all about personal computing going from local to global.

You may already be practicing some simple forms of cloud computing without even realizing it: by having purchase receipts sent to you by email rather than storing pieces of paper in a shoe box; by reviewing your bank statements via your bank's online banking service; by documenting your day on a social network rather than in a physical diary; by automatically uploading your snapshots to Google Photos. Not only are these important pieces of information no longer physical, they are no longer local. Even when you download an ebook to your specific Kindle device, you don't expect to lose the book when you lose the Kindle. Just conjure up another Kindle and your entire book library will once again become instantly available.

It's the Browser, Stupid!

I'm not calling you stupid, so please don't take offense. But I do want you to think about how you spend most of the time on your computer.

I bet most of your time is spent shopping online, banking online, booking hotels, emailing, Googling for information, and (for many of you) networking with your friends on Facebook. None of these activities requires a fully functional traditional PC, but all of them depend on your internet connection. If this is all you do with your computer then all you really need is a cheap and cheerful device that acts as the window on your online world. All you need is a chromebook.

Okay, so you also write documents and manage spreadsheets which require the full power of the Microsoft Office suite. Or do they? Have you checked out what the web-based Google Docs office suite can do recently, not to mention Microsoft's own online Office apps?

Computing Comes Full Circle

With the advent of cloud-based services, computing has (in a sense) come full circle.

In the early days of computing, all of the heavy duty processing took place on a central mainframe computer to which computer users "dialed-in" from dumb terminals via a telephone modem or their organization's corporate network.

As computer processors and memory became cheaper, it was possible for users to own their own fully functional computers that were not as dumb as the old dumb terminals and which were not limited by very slow dial-in connections to the centrally-controlled mainframe computers. This was the era of Microsoft Windows and (to a lesser extent) the Apple Macintosh.

With the advent of the internet, the pendulum once again swung back toward a world in which processing power and media storage has become centralised. Web browsers have taken on the task of the old dumb terminals, but the chromebooks and other computers that run those web browsers are not so dumb. And with the wide-scale adoption of fibre broadband and 4G, they're not so slow either.

Chapter Summary

The point of this first chapter has been to introduce you to the chromebook concept and its relevance to cloud computing. For many of you, this new way of working "in the cloud" may well be quite different from the traditional PC-based local computing that you may have experienced to date.

Welcome to a new way of working. And playing.

In many ways, computing has come full circle, back to the days when computing was controlled from some central computers accessed remotely. Now we've gone back to the future with chromebook computers accessing computing power in the cloud.

A Pixelbook Primer

While I've tried to make this book a generic as possible, and applicable to all chromebooks, I have mainly made use of the latest and greatest (at the time of writing) Google Pixelbook for this latest and greatest iteration of my book. So in this chapter I'd like to tell you about the Pixelbook peculiarities that make it oh-so special.

*You don't need a Pixelbook to make the most of this book! While a shiny new Pixelbook might be the icing on your (and my) cake, you can use any old or new chromebook computer to bake the cloud computing cake, so feel free to skip ahead to the chapter titled **Chromebook Installation and Initialization**.*

Still with me? Good. Now let's look at the Pixelbook in particular, focusing on the new features that may well work their way into other chromebooks in the not-too-distant future.

The Pixelbook Form Factor(s)

Don't know what a "form factor" is? It's just a technical term for the size and shape of a device; i.e. whether it's laptop or a tablet. The Pixelbook is actually both, so for the high price of the Pixelbook you're actually getting two devices in one: a chromebook computer and an Android tablet.

In the same way as Lenovo's once-innovative Yoga Book laptops, the Pixelbook screen can be bent right back to turn the Pixelbook laptop into a touchscreen tablet, and you can even turn it into a 'tent' midway to watch a movie.

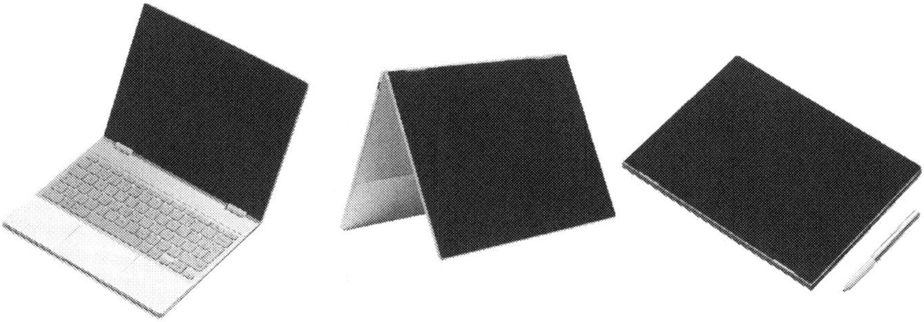

Having worked with many different types of laptops, tablets, and laptop-cum-tablets with detachable keyboards or screens (such as the Microsoft Surface line) I have found the all-in-one bend-right-back approach to be my favorite form factor by far. Put simply: as someone who works equally frequently with words and pictures, I wouldn't know when it was safe take a tablet on my travels without its keyboard, so the keyboard may as well be always attached.

The problem with tablets having always-attached keyboards, even ones that flip right over, is the added thickness of the folded device. The Pixelbook addresses this problem by apparently being the thinnest laptop ever made.

Tablet Touchscreen

The tablet touchscreen allows you to work equally well with words and pictures; not that the Pixelbook is the first - and certainly won't be the last - chromebook to take the touchy-feely approach.

Pixelbook Pen

If you're a creative type like me, you'll appreciate the Pixelbook Pen for picture-work precision.

Although Apple did away with the 'stylus' as the accepted input method when it invented the iPhone and iPad, I have always preferred the pen to the finger as the natural tool for taking notes, drawing pictures, and simply selecting things on a screen. You'll know what I mean if you have ever tried signing your name with your finger. I'm personally pleased that the Pixelbook Pen means fewer fingerprints on the screen, and pleased that the tilt support plus pressure sensitivity (and very little lag) provides an experience a lot like putting real pen to paper.

I'm particularly pleased that the pen doesn't need 'pairing' with the Pixelbook via Bluetooth or any other convoluted configuration. Just insert the battery, point at the Pixelbook screen, and you're ready to write. The only downside to the Pixelbook Pen is the lack of a slot to store it in or on the Pixelbook itself.

Configuring the Pixelbook Pen

You can use the Stylus section of the chromebook Settings to change the way the Pixelbook Pen works. In particular, you can enable the pen to be used to take notes even when your chromebook is locked, thus making the Pixelbook an always on-hand notebook.

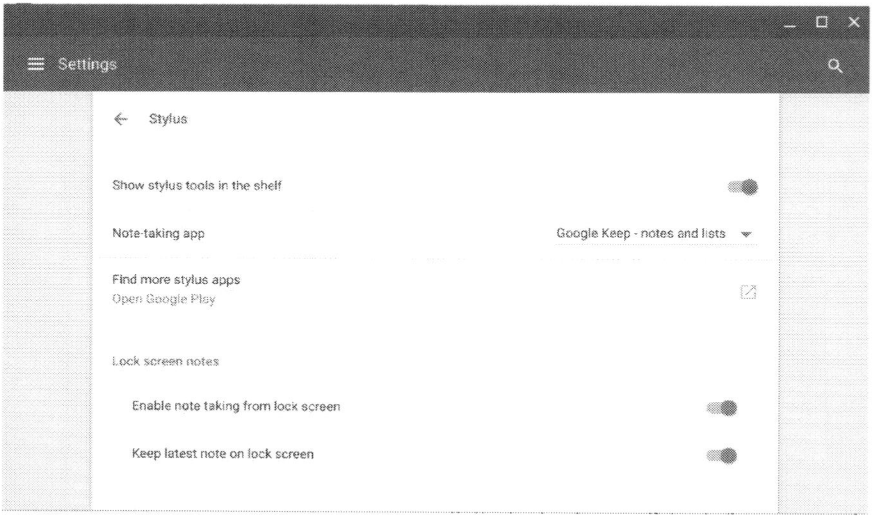

The way this works is that when you have locked your chromebook **(1 below)** the note-taking icon **(2)** appears at the top right of the lock screen, from where you can launch Google Keep (or another configured note-taking app) after which you will be notified **(3)** that you took a note on the lock screen:

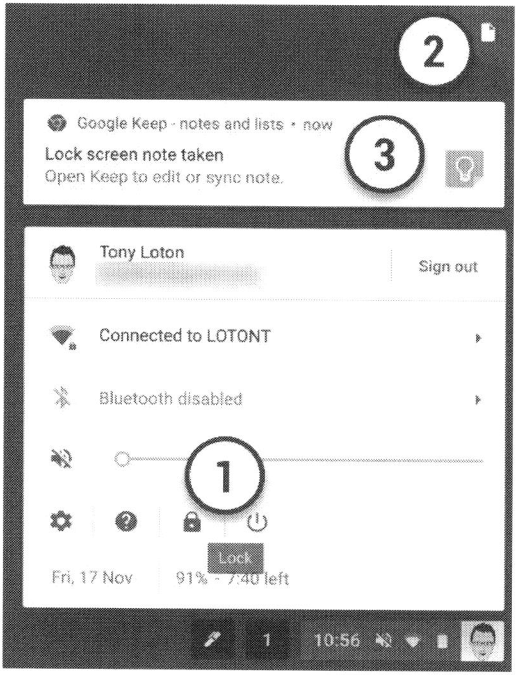

Working with the Pixelbook Pen

To some extent you can work anywhere with the Pixelbook Pen that you would usually work by pointing your finger (on a touchscreen) or moving and clicking with the trackpad cursor. But not all apps are created equal when it comes to the Pixelbook Pen.

For example, by applying an increasing amount of pressure I was able to create the following sketch in the Infinite Painter Android app:

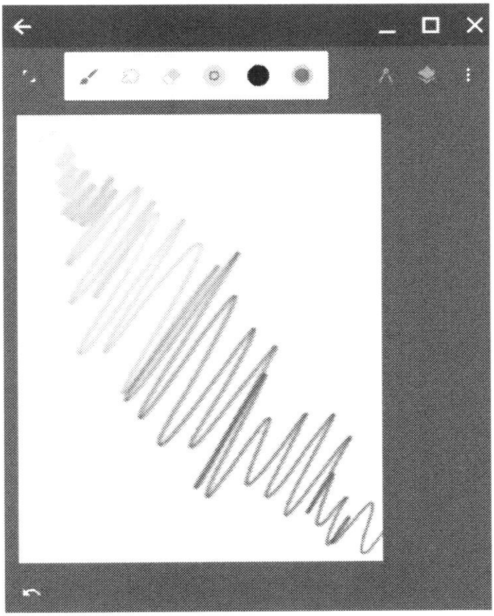

I wasn't able to achieve the same thing using my preferred Pixlr Editor online app because it doesn't recognize when I apply more pressure with the pen. It doesn't matter too much for most of the work I do, but artists might want to choose their preferred app more carefully for its Pixelbook Pen support.

By clicking the pen icon at the bottom-right of the Pixelbook screen you can change the way the pen works using the different "Stylus tools". As shown next, you can use the pen to magnify a section of the screen **(1)** or as a virtual laser pointer **(2)** when presenting to the public. The Pixelbook Pen also works with Google Assistant, which is my convenient segue into the next section.

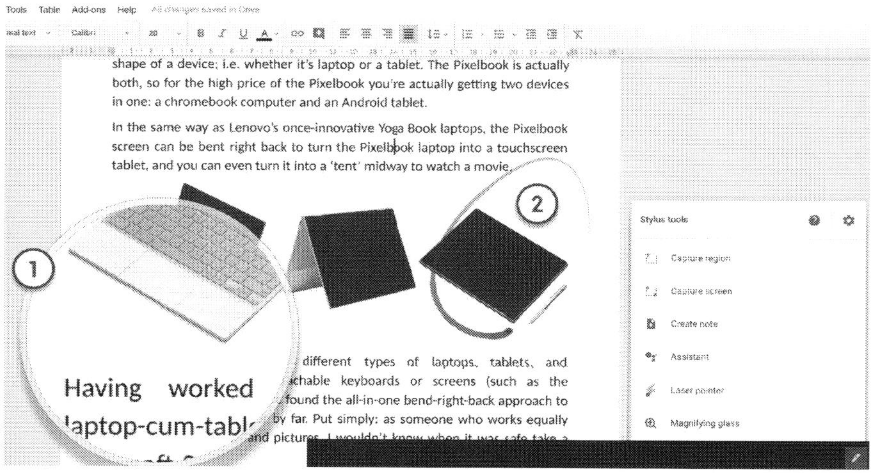

Google Assistant

For some time now we've been able to bark instructions at our mobile phones and have our questions answered by their built-in electronic assistants such as Siri (on Apple devices) and Cortana (on Microsoft machines). Now it seems that internet-connected home speakers are all the rage with their respective assistants such as Alexa on the Amazon Echo, and Google is in on this act too with its Google Home speaker that is driven by Google Assistant.

The Pixelbook is the very first – but certainly won't be the last – chromebook to feature the very same Google Assistant that can respond to your voice commands, so in this respect you might save (or have saved) yourself some money by employing your Pixelbook in the role of a Home speaker substitute...providing you don't close the lid.

One way in which the Assistant on the Pixelbook differs from the Assistant on your Android phone is in its support for the Pixelbook Pen, which will be my main focus in this Pixelbook Primer chapter. You can make the pen work in Assistant mode by choosing Assistant from the "Stylus tools" at the bottom of the screen.

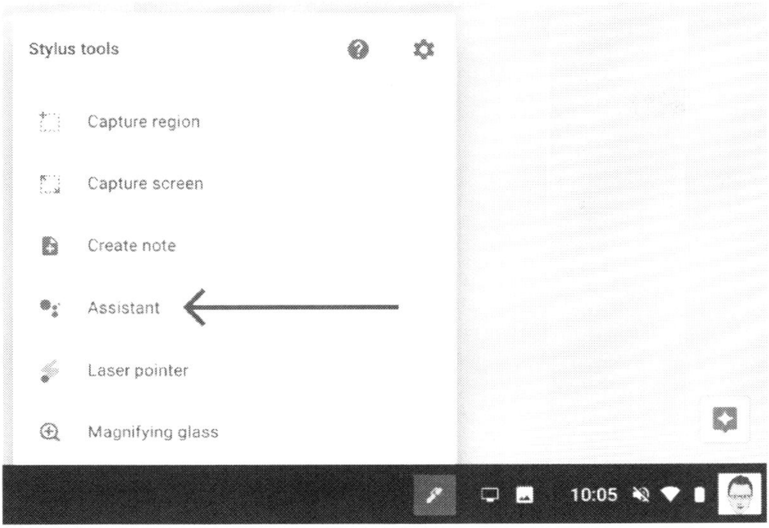

If you didn't already turn on the Assistant during the initial chromebook setup, you will now be prompted to do so. You'll need to accept that Google wants to watch your web and app activity as well as keeping track of your location, you can optionally train the Assistant to recognize your voice, and can choose to let the Assistant use what's on your screen to show you related info, apps and actions.

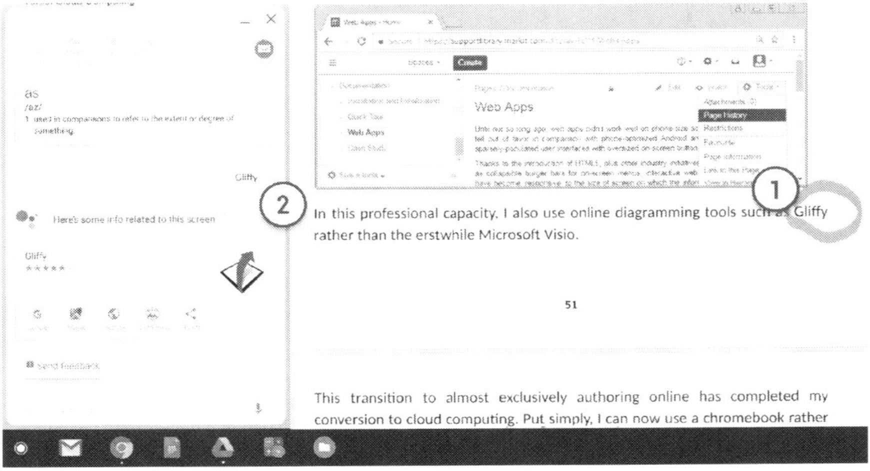

As an alternative to choosing the Assistant stylus tool from the on-screen menu, you can always put the pen into Assistant mode by pressing the button on the pen while circling something on the screen. In the example shown above, I wanted to find out more about the Gliffy tool that I mention in this manuscript, so I have circled the word Gliffy **(1)** to see a link to the software in the Assistant pop-up **(2)**. Personally, I find it much more useful simply to press the Assistant key on the chromebook keyboard and type a question such as "What is Gliffy?" so that Google gives me a much better answer.

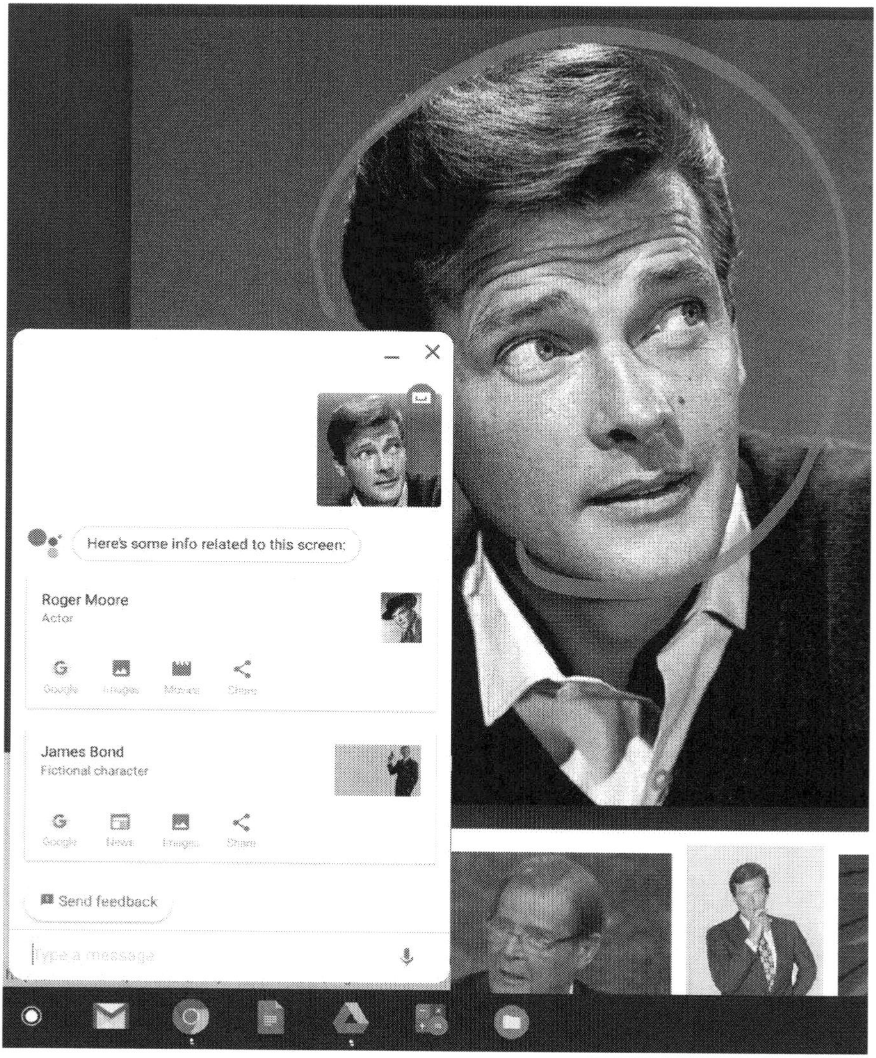

Where the Pixelbook Pen really comes into its own is by allowing me to circle an image to find out more information, which is not something I could achieve by typing. In the previous picture I have circled an image of an actor, which Google Assistant helpfully tells me is Roger Moore who played the fictional character James Bond in movies.

I should end my introduction to Google Assistant by telling you that you can also activate the Assistant by voice by saying “Okay Google” followed by your questions. While working in a coffee shop, I said “Okay Google, what’s this song?” to help me identify the song that was playing in the background. Google Assistant helpfully informed me that it was the song “Re-Wiring Easily” from the album “Salivating for Symbiosis” by Morning Teleportation. I never would have known.

Chapter Summary

During the development of this book I have used Google’s latest (at the time of writing) Pixelbook chromebook, and in this chapter I have introduced the Pixelbook peculiarities for the benefit of those of you who have bought or are thinking of buying one. In particular, I have told you about:

- Pixelbook form factors.
- Tablet touchscreen and Pixelbook Pen.
- Google Assistant

These peculiarities will likely not be so peculiar (i.e. unique) for very long as they become adopted by the more mainstream chromebook crowd.

Chromebook Installation and Initialization

In this chapter we'll open the chromebook box to see what's inside. Then we'll work through the installation and initialization steps of the initial setup.

What's in the Box?

What's in the box may differ depending on chromebook model you buy, but my Google Pixelbook box contained the following items:

- ➢ The Pixelbook.
- ➢ A USB charger and cable.

Okay, so there were also three slim slips of cardboard titled "Be safe", "Let's get started" and "Get to know your Pixelbook". The "Be safe" one contained all the small-print safety and warranty information that you'll probably never ever read. The other two were as follows:

Let's get started

This set of simple instructions simply instructs you to "Plug your Pixelbook in to charge", "Open your Pixelbook to turn it on", and "Follow the on-screen steps to finish setup" (with a warning that you'll need a Wi-Fi connection and a Google Account to do so).

Get to know your Pixelbook

This tri-fold piece of card helps you locate the various ports and buttons around the edge of the Pixelbook, shows you the four form factors for the device, and suggests you meet your Google Assistant at assistant.google.com.

You don't need to know any more about this if you didn't purchase a Pixelbook, but whichever chromebook you did buy will probably have a similar simple set of instructions to help you find your way.

Help!

If you need any more help at any point, you can simply click the Help icon as shown next.

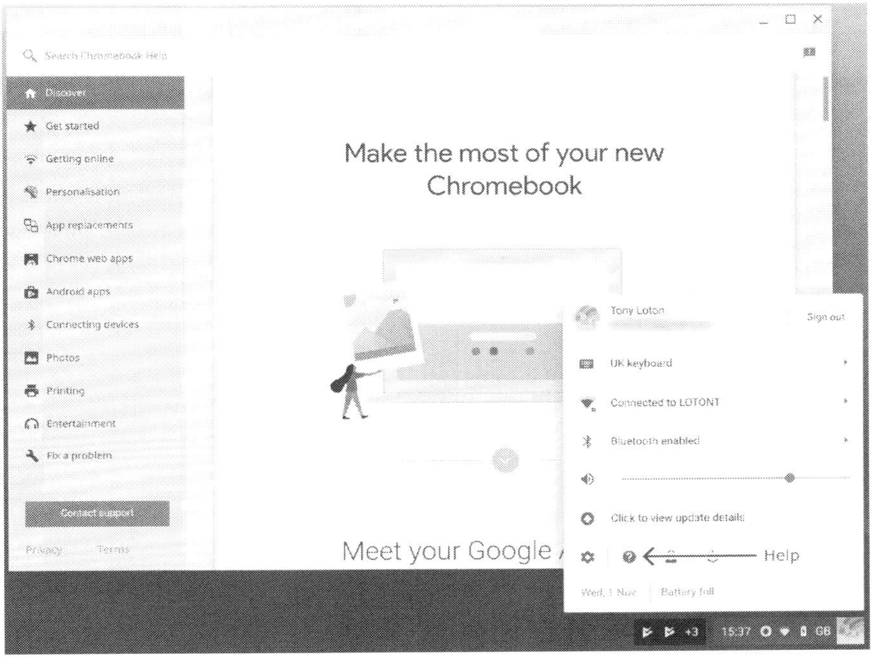

But we're getting ahead of ourselves, because you haven't set up your chromebook yet.

The Chromebook Initial Setup

Note that the evolving nature of technology means the steps described here may be slightly different when you come to set up *your chromebook*. Nonetheless, this rough sequence of events should give you a good idea of how the initial setup goes:

- ➢ The Welcome step allows you to select your language and access accessibility options including "ChromeVox (spoken feedback)", "Large mouse cursor", "High contrast mode", "Screen magnifier", and "On-Screen Keyboard".
- ➢ The "Connect to network" step invites (if not obliges) you to select a Wi-Fi network in order to complete the setup. I connected to my Android phone's hotspot.
- ➢ The "Google Chrome OS Terms" then have to be accepted, but you can opt out of "helping make Chrome OS better by automatically sending diagnostic and usage data to Google".
- ➢ The next step is to "Sign in to your Chromebook" using the email address of your Google Account. You'll already have a Google Account if you use

gmail or have an Android phone, and – if all else fails – you can "Create account" or use "Guest mode".

➢ You then have to accept the "Google Play Terms of Service", but you can opt out of automatically backing up Play app data to Google Drive (which I don't bother with) and letting Google's location service help apps find your location quickly and accurately (ditto). Don't worry if you make the wrong decisions, because you can always change your choices later.

➢ You can "Give your new Assistant permission to help" you by monitoring your Web & App Activity and your Location History. You can choose "NO, THANKS" if you don't want Big Brother to be watching you in these ways.

Powering On and Off

Think of your chromebook as more like your mobile phone, which goes from powered-on to standby (and back again) pretty much instantaneously. Just close the chromebook lid to switch off the screen and go into standby mode, and then flip it open again to resume working immediately.

Also like your mobile phone, you can properly power-off the chromebook by pressing the physical power button for a few seconds or by accessing the power menu by clicking at the bottom-right of the screen then selecting the power icon:

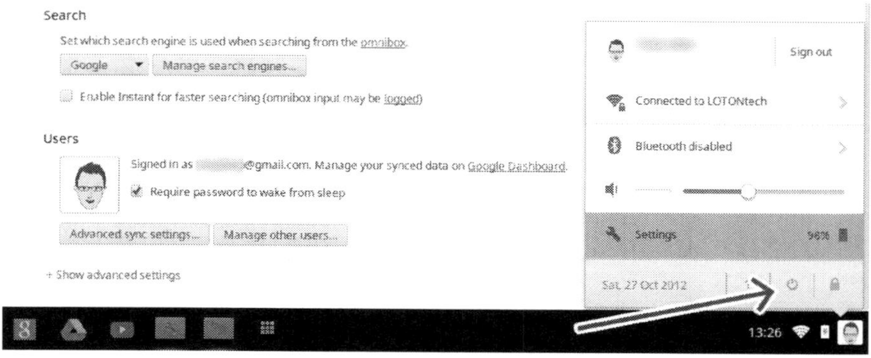

Chapter Summary

In this short chapter I have told you what you need to do to get started with your brand new chromebook, in the context of what I needed to do to get started with my brand new Google Pixelbook. In the next chapter we'll dig a little deeper into how to interact with a chromebook via the keyboard and (if available) touchscreen.

Chromebook Keyboard and Touchscreen

This chapter tells you how to interact with your chromebook via the keyboard and touchscreen.

Chromebook Keyboard

As you can see below, the chromebook keyboard is a regular QWERTY keyboard with the PC "function keys" (F1-F12) on the top row replaced by some dedicated chromebook keys.

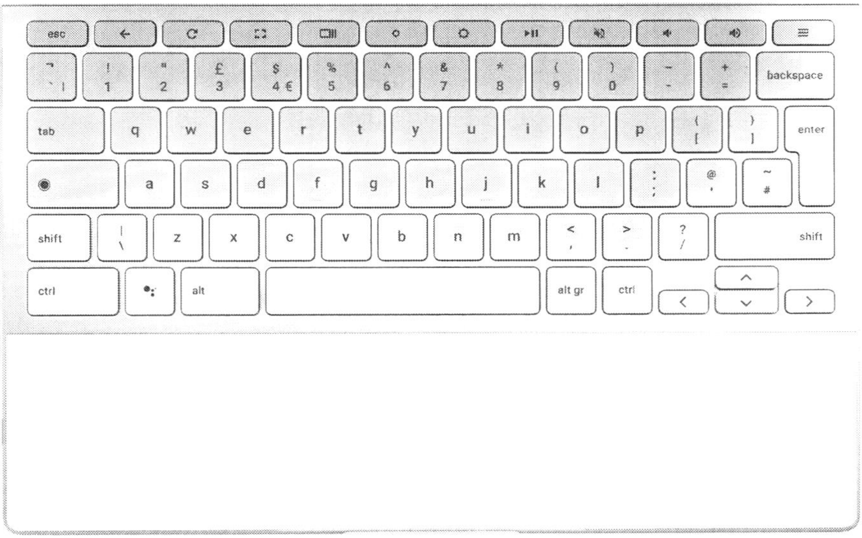

Most of the keys on the standard QWERTY keyboard work exactly as you would expect them to work on a traditional PC, Macbook or any other computer, so I won't waste your time by telling you what the keys such as **backspace** and **shift** do, nor the keys for brightness and volume.

There are some chromebook-specific keys that may be unfamiliar and deserve a special mention here:

 is the **back** key that takes you back to the previously-displayed browser page or acts like the back key on an Android phone (which may be important when using Android apps on your chromebook).

 is the **refresh** key that refreshes the currently-displayed browser page.

 is the **maximize** key that makes the browser fill the full screen. It can also be used to toggle the display mode between "mirrored" and "extended display" when your chromebook is attached to a big screen TV.

is the **switch window** key that allows you to switch between browser windows, which is particularly important when you have more than one of them maximized.

launches the system menu that shows info like Wi-Fi network connection and volume level.

is the Google Assistant key that allows you to initiate the assistant to answer your questions. On some older chromebooks this key will be a **search** key labelled with a spyglass icon.

is the launcher key that opens the app launcher, or at least it does so unless you have reconfigured the key to perform its traditional PC function as the Caps Lock key via the chrome://settings/keyboard-overlay page as shown here:

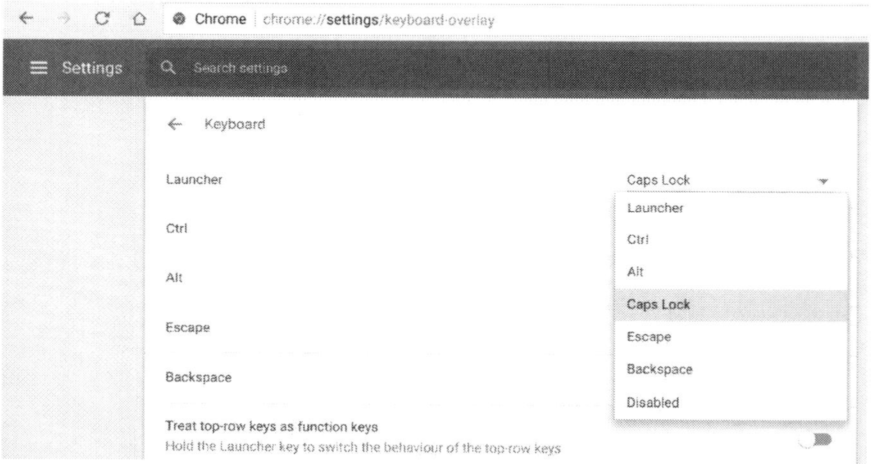

Note that in addition to the dedicated function keys, there are also some key combinations that perform specific tasks as detailed below.

ctrl + click a link : *Open the linked web page in a new browser tab, and also switch to the newly-opened tab if **shift** also pressed.*

ctrl + **switch window** key : *Captures a screenshot of what is currently displayed on the chromebook screen, and saves it as a Portable Network Graphics (.png) image in your Downloads folder. Pressing the **shift** key at the same time allows you to select a part of the screen to be captured.*

ctrl + tab : *Go to the next browser tab; or the previous tab if **shift** also pressed.*

ctrl + + : *Zoom in the current web page.*

ctrl + - : *Zoom out the current web page.*

ctrl + 0 (zero) : *Reset the zoom level.*

ctrl + 1, ctrl + 2 and so on : *Open the tab in the specified position.*

ctrl + a : *Highlights the entire contents on display, which can then be copied by pressing* ***ctrl + c*** *and pasted into another app by pressing* ***ctrl + v****.*

ctrl + d : *Adds the current web page to your list of bookmarked web pages, or bookmarks all pages if* ***shift*** *also pressed.*

ctrl + f : *Allows you to find (and highlight) specific text on the web page you are viewing.*

ctrl + g : *Find the next match, or the previous match if* ***shift*** *also pressed.*

ctrl + j : *Presents you with the contents of your Chrome browser downloads folder which can also be accessed by typing chrome://downloads/# into the browser omnibox (web address bar).*

ctrl + h : *Presents you with the contents of your Chrome browser history which can also be accessed by typing chrome://history into the browser omnibox.*

ctrl + k : *Invites you to perform a Google Search.*

ctrl + n : *Opens a new browser window, and pressing the* ***shift*** *key at the same time opens the window in incognito (untracked) mode.*

ctrl + o : *Allows you to select a file to open.*

ctrl + p : *Launches the Google Cloud Print dialog.*

ctrl + r : *Reload the current web page, and ignore the cached version if* ***shift*** *also pressed.*

ctrl + s : *Opens a dialog that allows you to save the current file; e.g. the web page you are viewing.*

ctrl + t : *Opens a new browser tab.*

ctrl + u : *Allows you to view the HTML source code for the current web page. If you don't know what this means, don't worry about it.*

ctrl + w : *Closes the current browser tab, whereas* ***ctrl + shirt + w*** *closes the current window.*

search key + 1 through to **search key + =** : *Simulates pressing the function keys F1 to F12, which may be useful when using the Chrome Remote Desktop to access a Windows PC remotely.*

Note that some of these key combinations only take effect if you have a browser window open. It's not a complete list of keyboard shortcuts, and you can see a more complete list here:

https://support.google.com/chromebook/answer/183101

Input Languages

You can change the available input languages within the advanced settings that you can access by typing chrome://settings into the Chrome browser's omnibox.

Chromebook Touchpad

You can plug a USB mouse into one of the USB sockets of your chromebook, and in the case of a desktop 'chromebox' you would have to do so, but the chromebook also has a touchpad or trackpad at the front of the keyboard which allows you to move the mouse cursor around the screen.

Gliding your finger around the pad moves the mouse cursor, and lightly tapping the pad (or pressing for a more responsive 'click') is equivalent to making a selection by clicking the left mouse button on a traditional mouse. A right-button click - which usually displays a context menu of additional options - is performed by tapping or pressing on the touchpad with two fingers. You can also place two fingers side-by-side on the touchpad and slide them up and down to scroll the screen contents up and down.

To drag an item on the screen, you press the touchpad with one finger and - without lifting that finger - slide another finger around the touchpad. You might think it would take two hands to do this, but with a little practice is possible to use just one hand.

Chromebook Touchscreen

While the original chromebook models did not sport a touchscreen, in the wake of the touchscreen-equipped Chromebook Pixel several touchscreen chromebooks were made available from manufacturers such as Acer. And in the second half of 2014, Lenovo launched a chromebook model with a screen that could flip through 360 degrees thereby transforming the chromebook from a traditional laptop form factor to a tablet-like form factor. As already alluded, the 2017 edition Google Pixelbook can also pull off this particular trick.

A touchscreen on a chromebook may still seem a little gimmicky since browser windows and their contents are not really optimized for touch screen operation, but I find it quite intuitive to scroll up and down a lengthy document by swiping my finger up and down the screen. This is one of several "gestures" that you can perform using your finger on the touch screen, with some of the others being:

- **Tap** to click.
- **Double-Tap** to double click.

- **Long Press** for a context click (like a right-click).
- **Scroll** (press and move your finger) to scroll or to drag and drop.
- **Flick** (tap and move your finger quickly) to scroll fast or switch pages.

Another gesture, which will be familiar to users of tablet computers such as the Microsoft Surface, is the ability to flick up from just off the bottom of the screen to reveal the launcher bar.

Users of other touchscreen tablets, laptops and smartphones will be familiar with at least one more touch gesture - pinch and zoom - which allows you to move two fingers together or apart on the screen in order to shrink or grow (contract or expand, zoom in or zoom out) the content shown on the screen.

Chapter Summary

In this chapter I have introduced you to chromebook interaction via the keyboard and touchpad, plus (on some models) the touchscreen. You will of course need something to interact with, and what you'll be interacting with is the Chrome OS desktop discussed in the next chapter.

Chrome OS Quick Tour

Chrome OS is the mainly browser-based operating system that controls the way your chromebook works. It's the equivalent of Android or iOS on your mobile phone, or Windows on a traditional PC. So you can think of this chapter as a quick-start conversion course that will help you reorient yourself if your previous PC ran on Microsoft Windows or another operating system.

A Brief History of Chrome OS

This time it's different. Or is it?

In the early days of the chromebook story it certainly looked like things would be quite different. Although chromebooks looked very much like Windows laptops, they didn't operate like them. The only program you could run on your chromebook was the Chrome web browser, and everything you did on the chromebook was via web pages running in the web browser. We could call this cloud computing in the purest sense.

But something interesting happened as the Chrome OS operating system evolved over the course of a few years. It started to look more and more like a traditional laptop or desktop operating system such as Microsoft Windows or Mac OS, at least from the user's perspective. First a PC-like file explorer was added, with the ability to play media files locally without an Internet connection. Then came a familiar desktop that can display multiple browser windows and which has a familiar application bar or 'shelf' at the foot of the screen. Finally, the ability to run Android apps was added to Chrome OS.

In many ways these evolutions were necessary because (to be frank) many potential purchasers of chromebooks found them to be just "too different" and too limiting despite looking superficially the same as traditional laptops. In some ways it saddened me slightly that the original pure cloud computing ethos had been watered down, but the chromebook is still the closest you will come to a true cloud computer.

Chrome OS Desktop

In the first versions of the Chrome OS, the screen would show a full-screen web browser... and that was all. The Chrome OS user interface has now evolved to resemble a PC desktop-style display that can show several browser WINDOWS (see below) with separate TABS, plus ANDROID APP(s). At the bottom of the screen you will find the LAUNCHER (to launch apps), a SHELF (to see which apps are running, and to pin some there for easy access), and a STATUS area (for at-a-glance information).

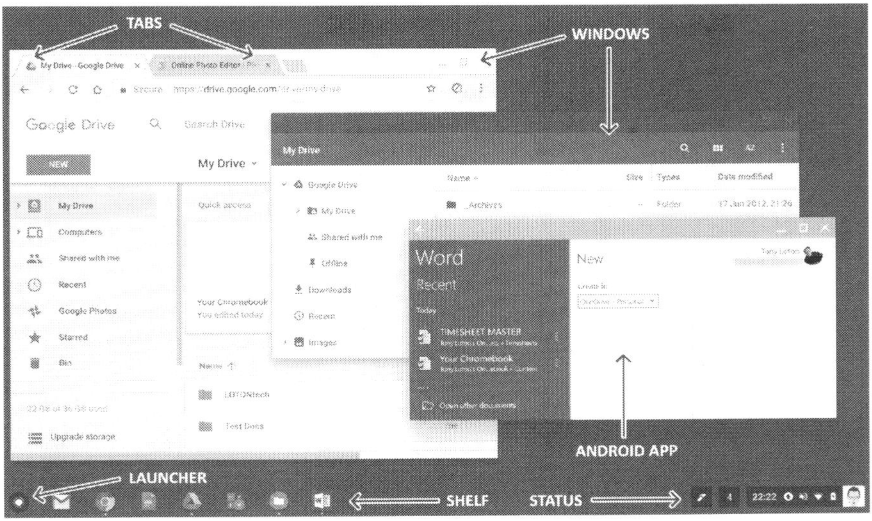

Browser Windows and Tabs

Although you can view separate web pages in entirely separate browser windows, most modern browsers (including Chrome) allow you to have different web pages displayed in different tabs within the same browser window. Some windows, such as the one for the Files app shown above, don't look like web browser windows at all.

When you have maximized your web browser and other app windows, you can easily see them all and switch between them by pressing the "switch windows" key:

Android Apps

Starting officially with the Pixelbook, but trialled in 'beta' for some time beforehand, Chrome OS now supports Android apps that run in resizable windows (if so optimised) when the Pixelbook is in laptop mode. Those same Android apps run in full-screen mode when the Pixelbook takes its tablet form.

In the earlier picture, I chose to show the Android app for Microsoft Word, and you'll read more about Android apps later.

App Launcher and Shelf

Across the bottom of the desktop you will find a horizontal shelf to which you can 'pin' your favorite apps, and you can see the full list of your web apps - plus any installed Android apps - by selecting the 'Launcher' icon at the bottom-left of the screen. Or press the Launcher key on the keyboard. You should see something like this:

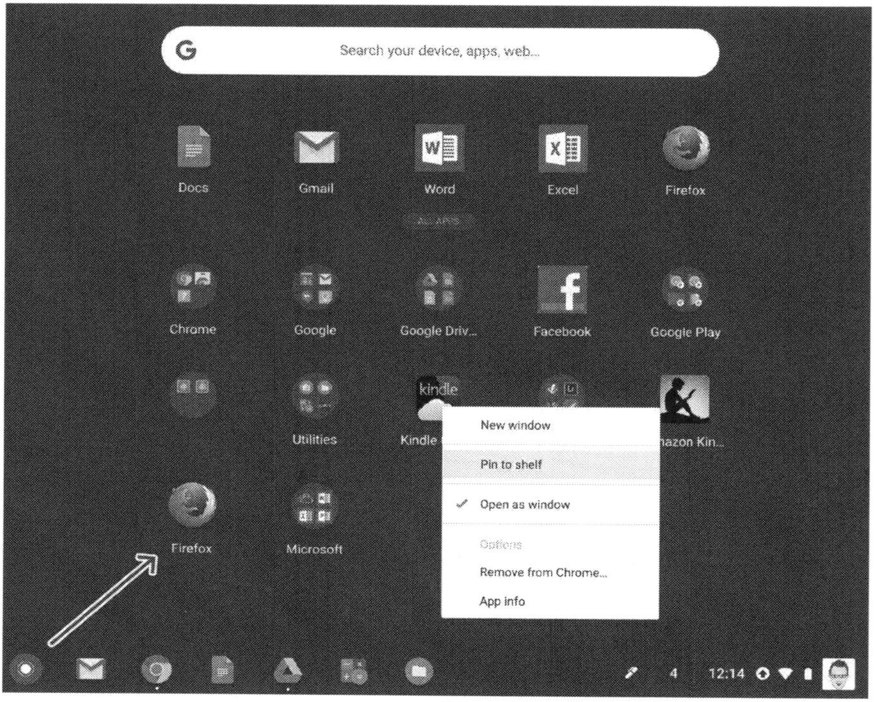

As well as launching an app from the launcher by left-clicking (or tapping), you can also display a context menu by right-clicking (or long-pressing) an app such as the Kindle app as shown above. This context menu allows you to pin apps to the bottom-of-screen shelf for easy access, or to configure apps to open in their own windows rather than in browser tabs. You can also move the app launcher icons around by clicking, holding, and dragging them around. And just like on your Android phone, you can drag app icons onto each other to create groups such as the "Microsoft" group I have created in the previous picture.

Shifting the Shelf

While I have described the shelf as being at the bottom of the screen, it is possible for you to shift the shelf by right-clicking on the desktop and choosing the "Shelf position" option to move it (for example) to the left or right of the screen. You can also specify whether the shelf should be always on display or hidden until you move the mouse pointer into the shelf area at the bottom (usually) of the screen.

Status Area

At the bottom-right corner of the screen sits the status area that displays a clock, Wi-Fi signal indicator, battery icon and your Google profile picture. It is from this area that you will also access incoming notifications (left picture below), and by clicking the cog icon you can choose which apps are allowed to post notifications (right picture below).

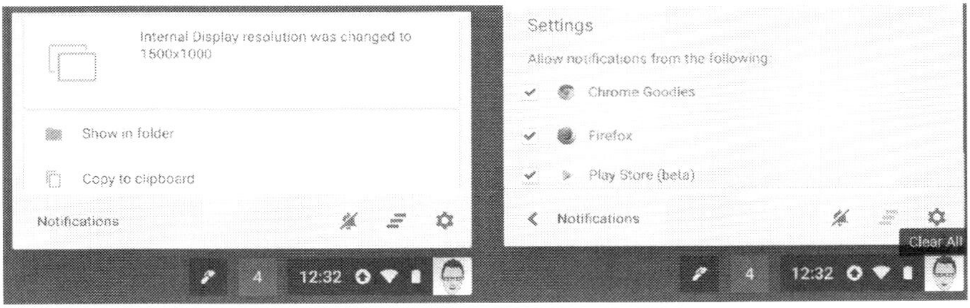

Settings

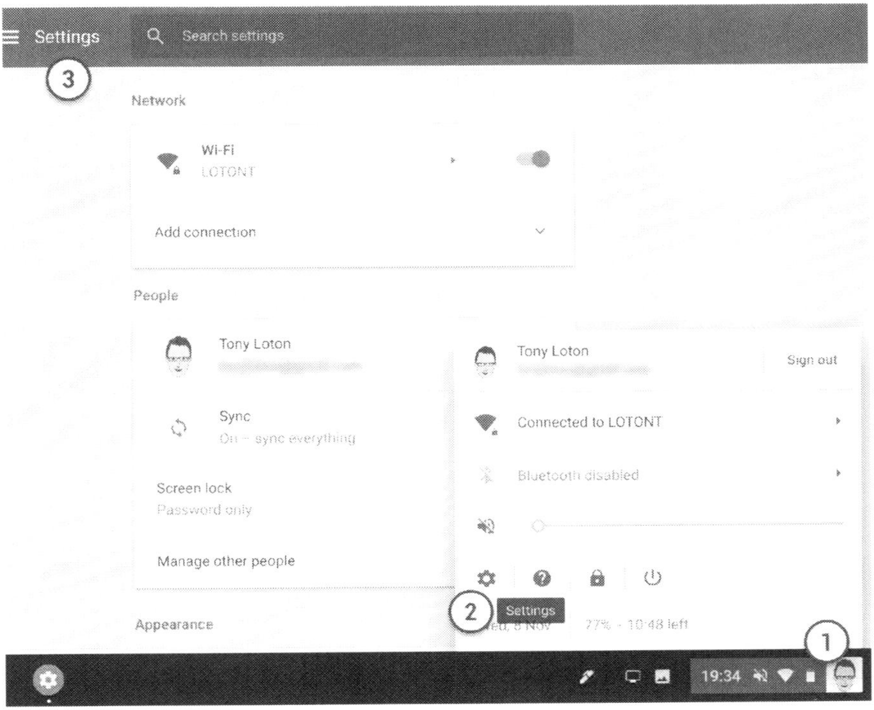

As shown above; by clicking in the status area **(1 above)**, then clicking the Settings cog icon **(2)**, you can access your Settings such as the current Wi-Fi connection. Most of the settings should be self-explanatory, but in the course of this book I will pick out a few of them for special mention in specific contexts.

Files

You can launch the Chrome OS file manager by selecting the Files app icon as shown next. In this file manager window you will see the available data drives or file storage locations listed in the left-hand column, which will typically include your Downloads folder (where documents will be placed when downloaded from the web), your Google Drive (which is the online storage linked to your Google account), and any external drives such as a USB stick or SD card you have inserted into your chromebook. You can also "Add new services" to connect up with other file systems such as Dropbox.

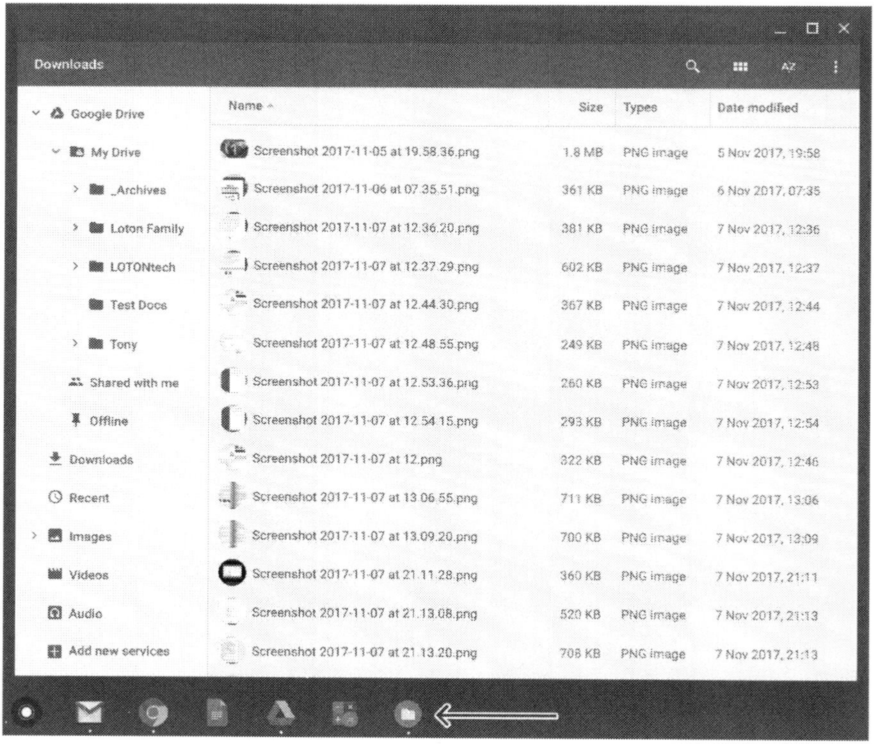

At the top of the Files app you can click an icon to switch the view from a list to a set of thumbnail images, and you can do all the things you would expect to do with a file manager app such as moving files from one folder to another. To copy a file to another location, right-click (or two-finger tap) the required file to launch its context menu and choose the Copy option, then browse to the desired destination folder before right-clicking again and choosing the Paste option to deposit the file.

The context menu **(1 below)** for any given file also allows you to perform various actions on a selected file—such as View (for a PDF) or Open (for a Google document). With a file selected you can also OPEN it **(2)** using applicable apps, or share it **(3)** using compatible apps including – in this case – the Microsoft OneDrive Android app which I have installed on my chromebook.

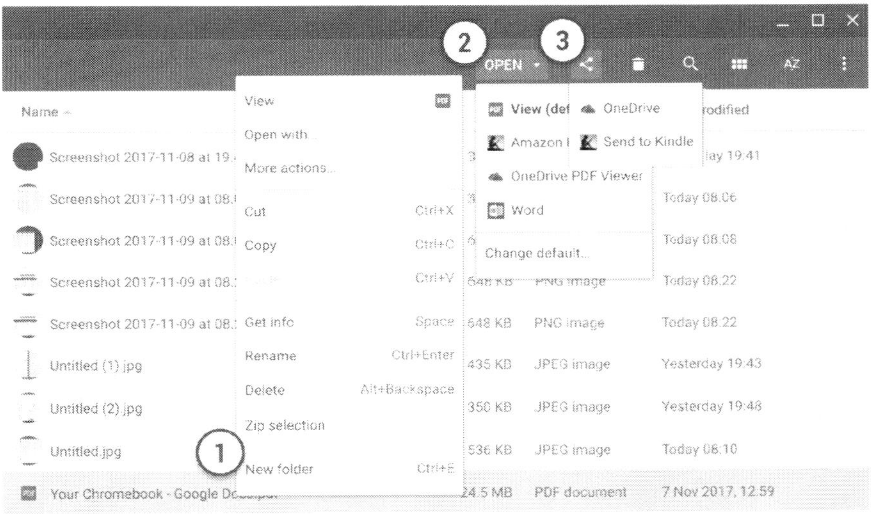

Dependence on the Downloads Folder

When working in the cloud via the Chrome web browser, you may never need to explicitly access your local files via the Files app at all. For example, it is perfectly possible to open an image in the Pixel Editor web app direct from your Google Drive, and to save it back there again.

However, not all web apps and websites are equal when it comes to accessing your Google Drive, in which case you'll find yourself using the Downloads folder as a temporary staging post for getting files from one web app to another. The following picture shows me downloading this book's manuscript as a Microsoft Word document **(1)** to the Downloads folder **(2)** so that I can then upload it to the Amazon Kindle publishing platform **(3)**:

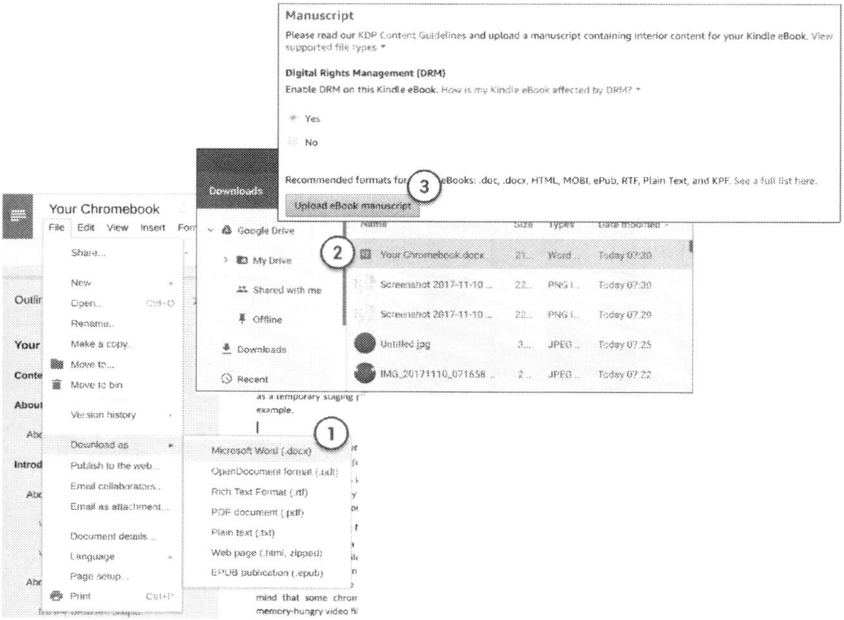

You might also like to know that any screenshots you take by pressing the **ctrl + switch windows** key combination will be deposited automatically in the Downloads folder for you to upload to wherever you want them, which in my case usually means uploading to the Pixlr Editor.

Opening and Playing Media Files

The chromebook has a basic multimedia player that allows you to play songs and movies from the Files app, whether these are on an inserted USB stick or SD card or have been downloaded to your Downloads folder. You don't need to be connected to the internet in order to play these media files, but keep in mind that some chromebooks have limited local storage space for storing memory-hungry video files for offline access.

In the following picture I have chosen the default "Open with Audio Player" option for a song I downloaded from my Amazon Music collection. You can see it playing in the media player at the bottom of the screen:

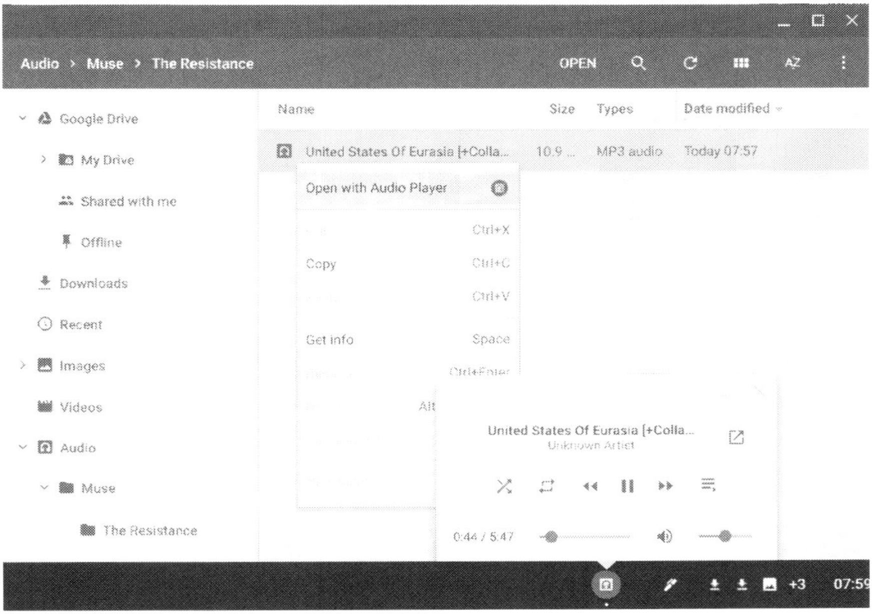

Basic Image Editing

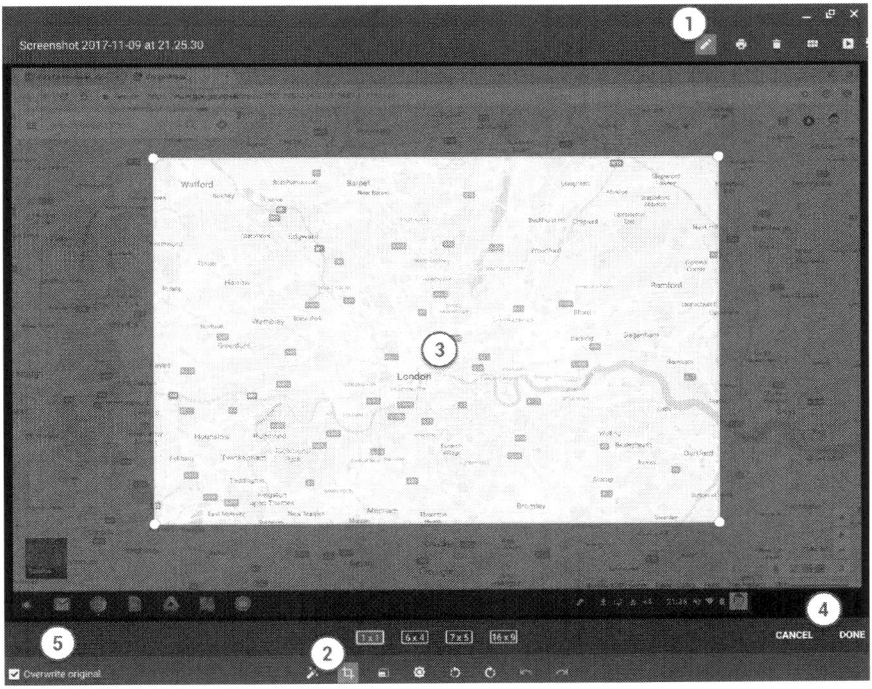

There is also a basic image editor that allows you to perform simple functions like cropping an image, changing its brightness, or rotating left or right. To edit an image, just "Open with Gallery" from the Files app, then click the pencil icon **(1 above)**, choose the cropping tool **(2)**, select the area of interest **(3)**, and click DONE **(4)**. Oh, and I should remind you to uncheck the "Overwrite original" checkbox **(5)** if you want to keep the original image intact.

If your image editing requirements extend beyond what this app can do, you might like to take a look at the Pixlr Editor web app that is available in the Chrome Web Store and at pixlr.com/editor/. If you have installed this app, you will be able to send an image file directly to Pixlr from the file manager by right clicking the file name and choosing the "Open with..." option followed by "Pixlr".

Moving Documents and Other Files from PC to Chromebook

Those of you who are transitioning from a traditional Windows PC to a chromebook will want to transfer your existing documents and other files from your old device to your new one.

One way you might do this is by using a USB drive as the transfer medium: insert it into your PC and copy the files out, then insert it into your chromebook and copy the files in. For some media files such as music or movies that you wish to play locally on your chromebook when offline, this may make some sense, providing you take account of the chromebook's likely much smaller hard disk compared with that of your PC.

The other way, which is much more cloud-computing-friendly, is not to transfer your files from one machine to the other at all. Instead, you would upload the files from your old PC to your new Google Drive online storage area, from where they will be accessible from your chromebook and from any other Internet-connected device. The easiest way to do this is with the Backup and Sync utility at g.co/drive/backupandsync.

Files App vs. Google Drive

The Google Drive app (or the web site at drive.google.com) and the Files app both provide access to exactly the same files, which means that - like almost everything else on a chromebook - there is more than one way of doing exactly the same thing. Or in this case doing different things with the same file, depending on how you access it.

The next two images show what happens when you right-click or two-finger-tap an image file in the online Google Drive vs. what happens when you do exactly the same thing via the Drive folder of the chromebook's Files app. Notice the different sets of available actions:

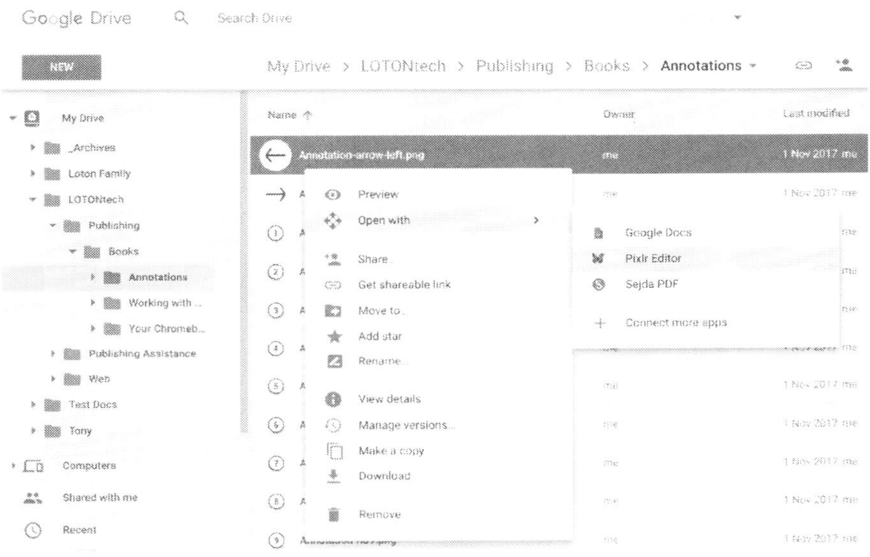

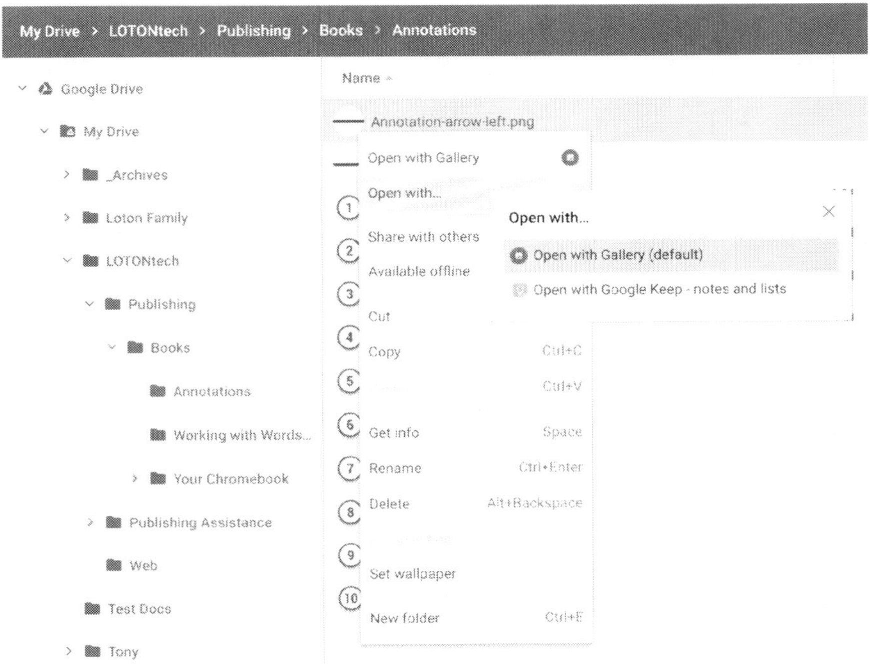

You might wonder why the difference, so you should think of it like this:

The Files app allows you to access your recent Google Drive files whether or not you are connected to the internet, and if you're not connected to the internet then you wouldn't expect to be able to access either the file's version history or the online Pixlr Editor web app. So those options only make sense when accessing a file from Google Drive online.

In summary, the Files app allows you to access Google Drive which stores your files safely (i.e. backed-up) in the cloud while also making your most recent files available offline when you're disconnected from the cloud. This brings me to...

Offline Access to Files

Although chromebooks were originally intended to be online-only computers (and I actually prefer it that way), over the years it has become possible to do more and more with chromebooks when disconnected from the internet. Many apps can work when offline, especially now that Chrome OS supports Android apps, and it is also possible to access files offline via the Files app.

While your chromebook can't possibly store copies of all your Google Drive files locally (unless you don't have that many) it will cache the most recent files you have been working on so that they are available offline.

You can edit Google Docs offline, but with certain limitations. For example, you can insert images from your chromebook's Downloads folder or from local copies of your Google Drive files, but you can't insert an image from a web address URL or from your online Google Drive. As a concrete example, you can see here that some of the images I might choose to insert are grayed-out because they have not been cached as local copies on my chromebook:

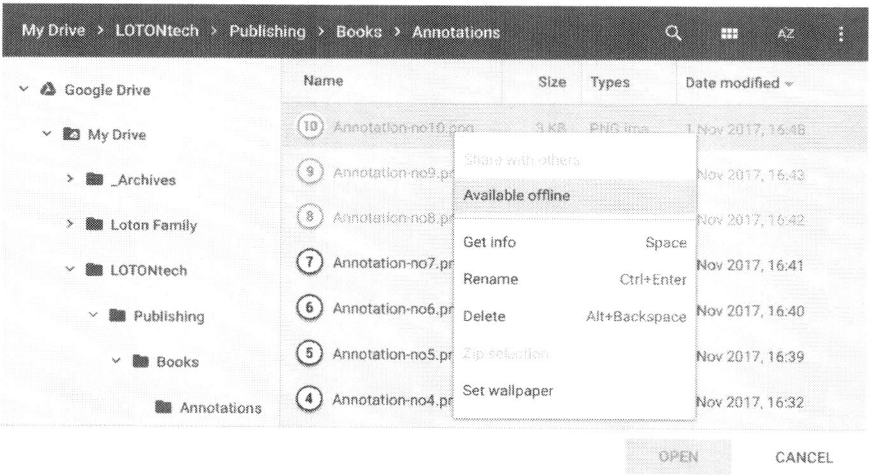

As shown above, from the context menu you can make any of those files "Available offline" from the next time you have an internet connection. If you ever feel that the offline files are taking up too much space in the chromebook's local storage, you can free up space by deleting the files via the the "Storage management" section of the chromebook Settings:

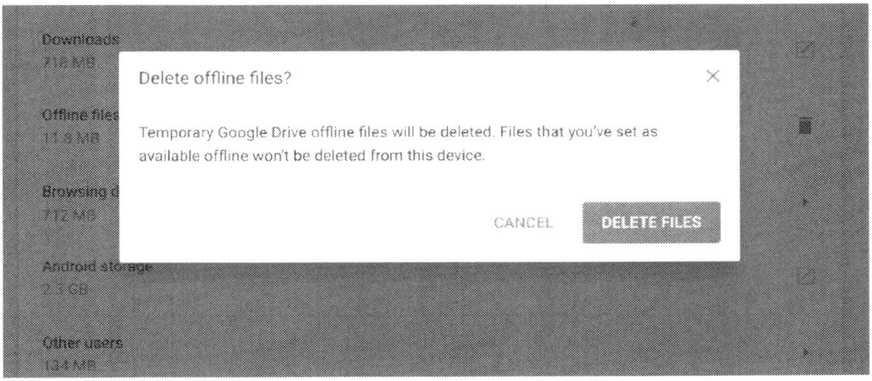

In this case, any file which you have explicitly enabled to be available offline will not be removed from your chromebook and will still be available offline:

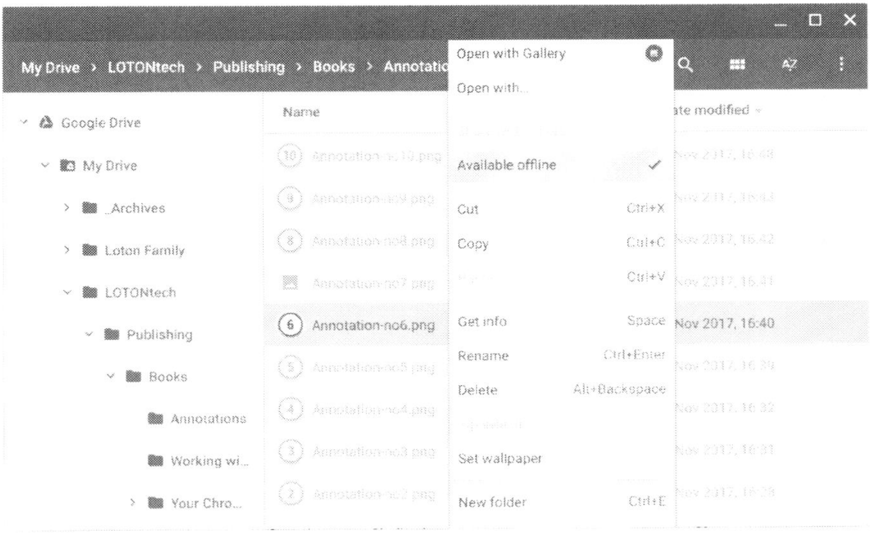

Chapter Summary

In this chapter I have told you what you need to know initially about interacting with the Chrome OS, whether this be:

- Working with windows, tabs, and apps of the desktop.
- Accessing the system status and settings.

- Finding and manipulating your files.
- Making files available to work on when offline.

Working with the Web Browser and Web Apps

Chrome OS has always been based primarily on the Chrome web browser, so in this chapter I focus on the web browser and the web apps that run within it.

Working in the Web Browser

The main (and possibly only) program you'll use on your chromebook is the Chrome web browser. I won't cover all the technical ins and outs of Chrome, but I will tell you what you need to know - and no more - in order to help you get going on your cloud computing journey. Even if you've never used the Chrome browser before, you will most likely have already used one of the other web browsers such as Internet Explorer, Mozilla Firefox, Opera, or Safari. They all do essentially the same job, and they all work in pretty much (but not exactly) the same way.

The Chrome browser is launched via the multicolored circular icon:

Tabs and Windows

You are probably already familiar with the fact that the Chrome browser allows you to open separate web pages in separate browser tabs.

This ability to open web pages in separate tabs within a single browser window was a great advance when first introduced to PC web browsers, because it saved you from launching the web browser program multiple times. Nevertheless, it is sometimes useful to have entirely separate browser sessions running, with different arrangements of tabs in each one, so that (for example) you can open all your email message tabs in one window and all your document tabs in another window. For this reason, the Chrome OS allows you to launch separate browser windows and switch between them using the dedicated **switch window** key (shown below) on your chromebook keyboard. Pressing it multiple times will cycle through your various browser windows.

Bringing the two ideas of separate tabs and separate windows together, you will be interested to know that you can "tear off" a browser tab to become a separate browser window. See here how I am tearing a tab from a browser window to become a window in its own right:

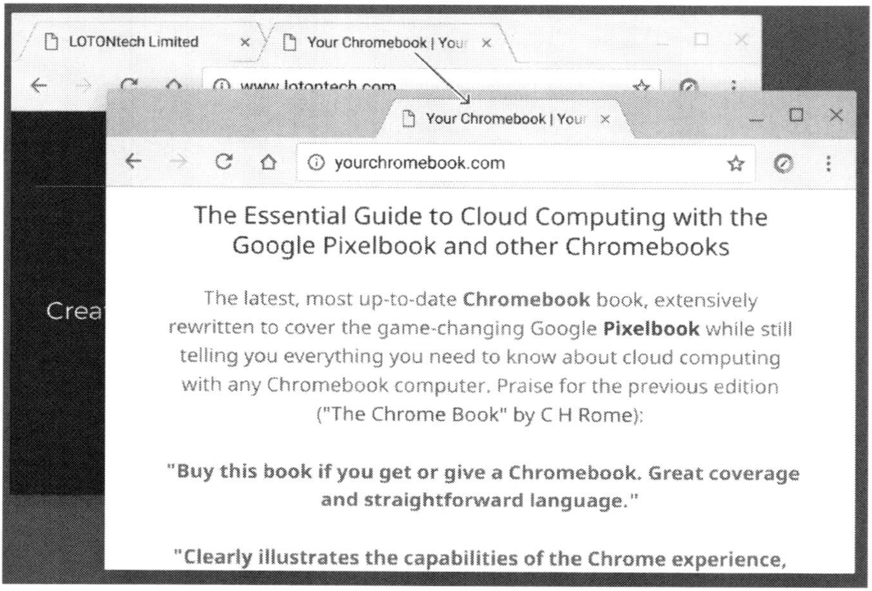

In pre-Chrome web browsers there was an address bar across the top into which you could type a web address Uniform Resource Locator (URL) such as www.yourchromebook.com. In Chrome, this address bar was renamed the *omnibox* to reflect the fact that you can enter some search text as an alternative to entering a web address. The need to enter direct web addresses has in any case been lessened by the ability to bookmark your favorite web pages (discussed in the next section) and to install web apps which in many cases are simply web shortcuts in all but name. *For some reason, probably sheer habit, I still prefer typing entire web addresses such as docs.google.com into the address bar / omnibox.*

To the left of the omnibox there are two arrows:

- The left-pointing arrow takes you back to the last page you were on before you clicked through to the current page, and the page before that one, and so on.
- The right-point arrow that takes you forward through those pages until you once again reach the current page. Back to the future, you might say.

Bookmarks

From "Customize and control Google Chrome" menu **(1)** you can select the Bookmarks option **(2)** to see your bookmarks, or "Show bookmarks bar" **(3)** so that the bookmarks become visible at the top of the browser **(4)**:

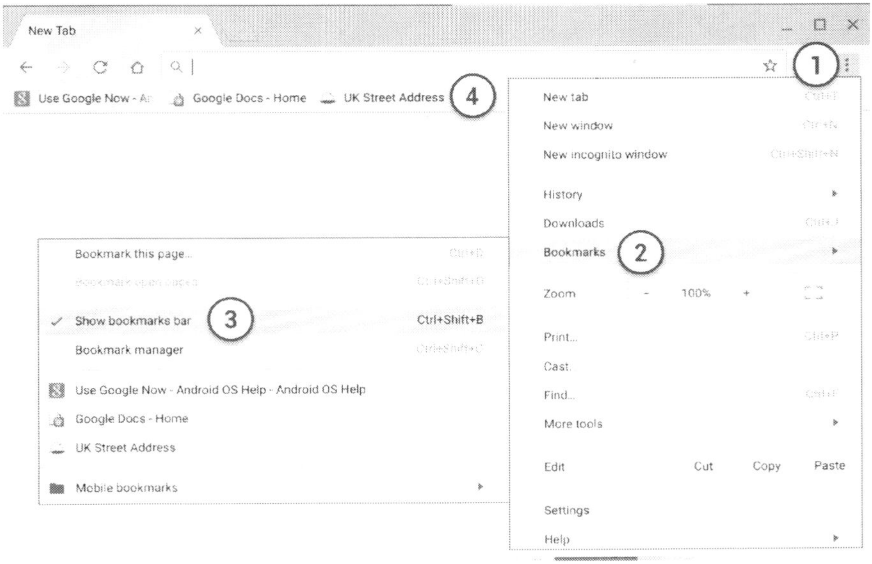

Just as in any web browser, you can bookmark your favorite web pages so that you can launch them at the click of a mouse or with a tap of the touchpad. You can add a bookmark for the web page you are currently viewing by clicking the star icon to the right of the browser address bar or by pressing the **ctrl+d** key combination.

Browsing History

As you browse the web, Chrome keeps track of the web pages you have visited. This can make it easier for you to return to those pages, it can make them quicker to load next time, and it can help Chrome to recover in the unlikely event that the web browser crashes.

You can view your web history by typing chrome://history into the omnibox, and you can clear down this history by clicking the "Clear browsing data" button. If you don't want your history to be tracked at all (I won't ask why) then you should open an incognito window or tab in the first place.

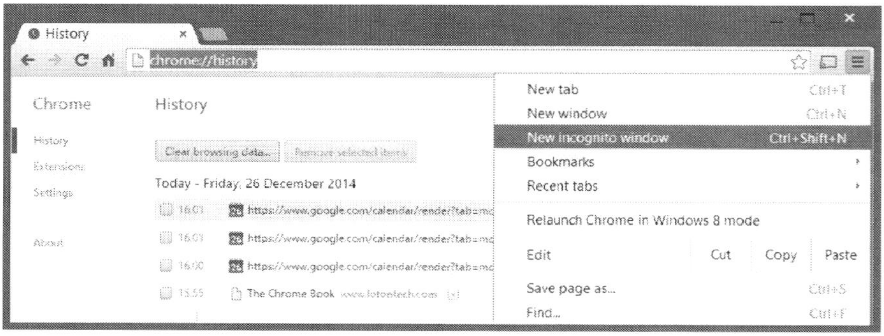

You can't see it in this picture, but when I took the screenshot it actually included the indication "Showing history from your signed-in devices", which brings me to...

Signing In to Chrome

Where it gets really interesting with the Chrome web browser is when you are signed in to your chromebook or Android device, or when you similarly "sign in" to the Chrome web browser on your PC as shown here:

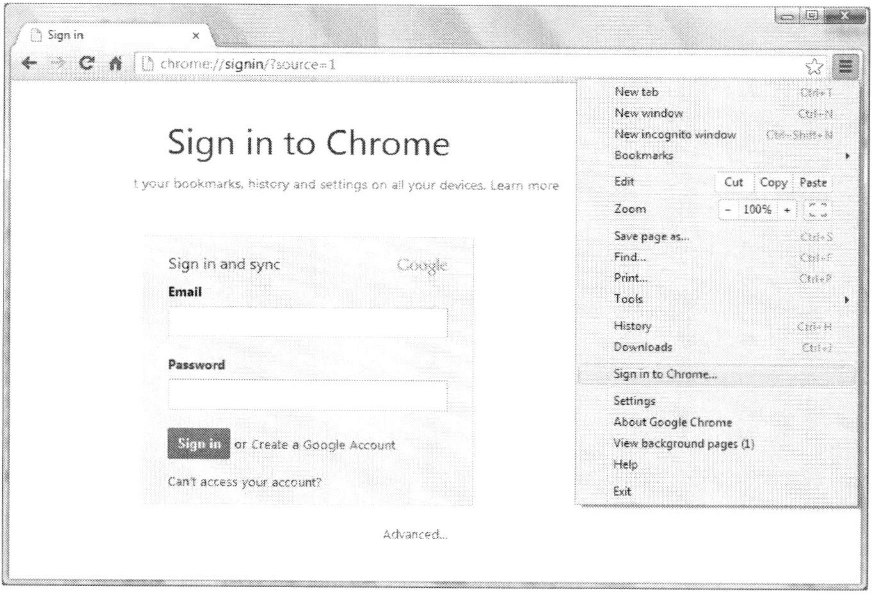

Your bookmarks and browsing history will now follow you to any device on which you sign into Chrome.

Browser Settings

You can access your Chrome browser settings either by selecting Settings from the pull-down menu or by typing chrome://settings into the browser address bar, or (on a chromebook) by clicking your user picture at the bottom-right of the screen and selecting Settings.

The settings you can view and configure will depend on whether you're running the Chrome browser on a PC or on a chromebook. On a chromebook these settings refer to your settings on the actual device, so in this case they will include Device settings to do with the touchpad, keyboard and display.

Some of the more interesting settings can be found by clicking the Advanced link at the foot of the settings page; for example: the settings for the "Google Cloud Print" facility or the options to "Factory Reset" or "Powerwash" your chromebook.

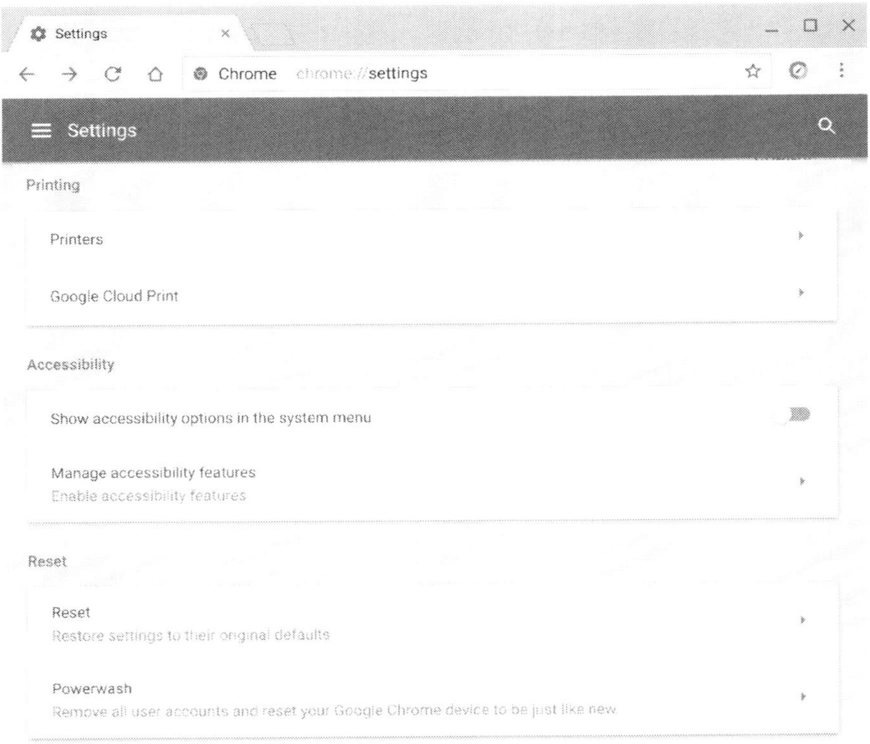

Working with Web Sites

Via a chromebook or the Chrome browser running on your PC, you can access any web site that you ever did: your internet banking web site, a social network such as Facebook, and so on. When you install the Facebook app from the

Chrome Web Store (discussed later), you are really only installing a shortcut to the Facebook web site at www.facebook.com.

QuickBooks Online

Don't underestimate what you can do with websites and website apps. For example, I run my company using Intuit's online version of its QuickBooks Online accounting suite at qbo.intuit.com (or via its installable app icon).

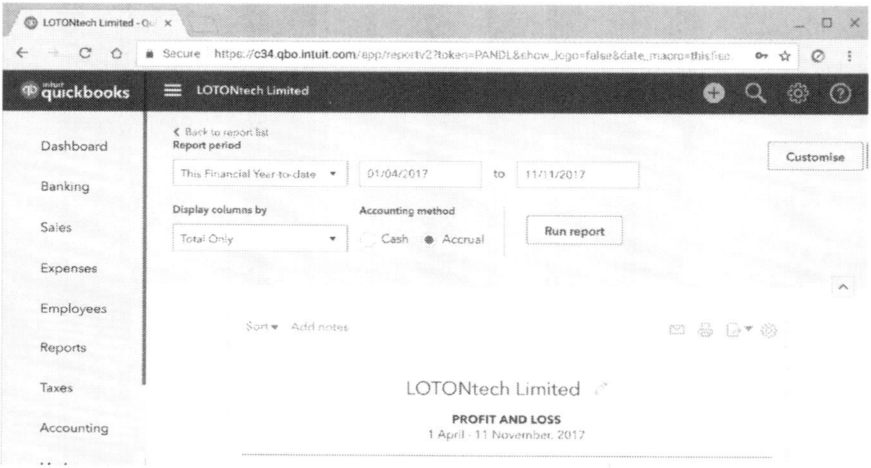

Kindle Cloud Reader

Another "website" app is Amazon's Kindle Cloud Reader that you can access by installing the app icon or by simply visiting the website at www.amazon.com/cloudreader. This app allows you to access your Kindle book library from any device (including a chromebook) that runs the Chrome web browser. No dedicated Kindle device or smartphone app is required.

Here is a picture of the Kindle Cloud Reader in action in the Chrome browser:

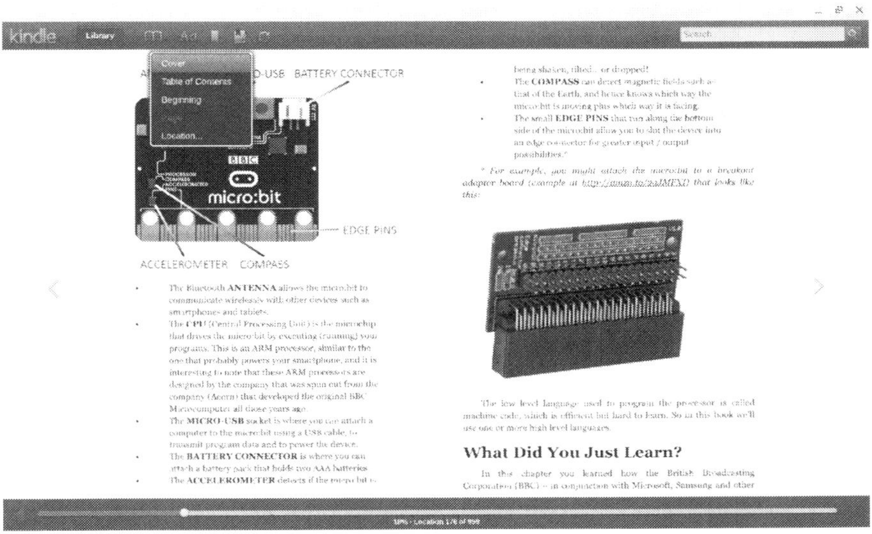

The great thing about this website / app is that it works when you are offline. Whenever you access one of the books in your Kindle library, it is automatically downloaded so that you can read it even when you are offline. You can also purposefully download a book, with a view to reading it later offline.

At this point it is worth reminding you than the alternative to building up your Kindle book library is to build up your Google Play Books library, as will be demonstrated later. On balance I prefer the Google Play reading experience, because most books can be viewed in PDF mode as they would appear when printed, rather than solely in the flowing-text mode that re-routes the text (not always that nicely) according to the size and orientation of your screen.

Pixlr Editor

As someone who engages in creative pursuits, for example designing book covers, a good image editing application is essential for me. But there really is no need for me to invest in the bona fide complete Adobe Photoshop application, therefore previously I have relied on the free PAINT.NET Windows application for my image editing needs. Obviously I couldn't use this particular program on a chromebook that doesn't run Windows programs at all, so I had a real requirement to find a good image editing application in the Chrome Web Store.

I found exactly what I needed in the form of the Pixlr Editor web app, which looks and feels remarkably like the PAINT.NET application that I was already used to, and which serves all my needs for image editing including manipulating multi-layered images. Here I am using the Pixlr Editor to manipulate the very picture that I just inserted into this book:

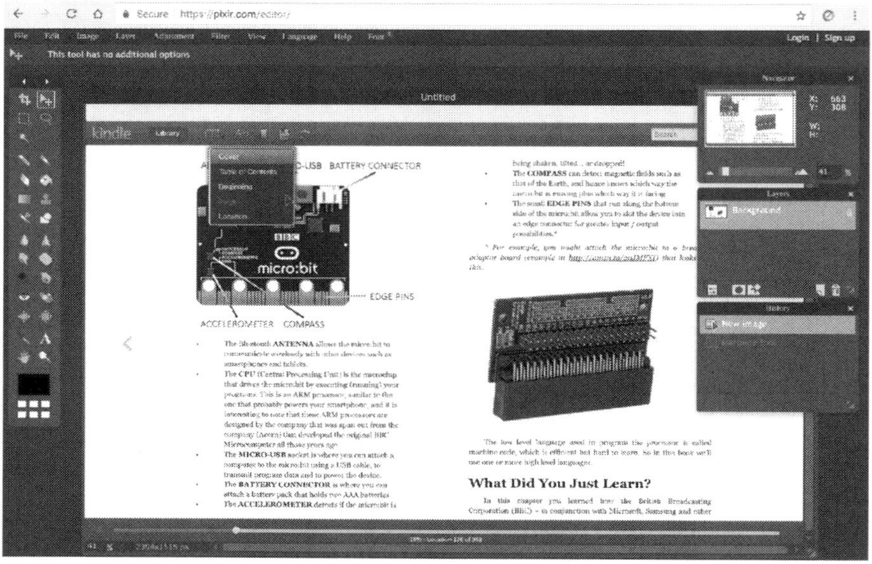

Confluence

In my professional life I often work with corporations as a technical writer. For many years this meant working with Word or another Windows-installed technical authoring tool such as Madcap Flare. Since 2016, for me it has meant working almost entirely within the web-based Confluence content authoring application pictured here.

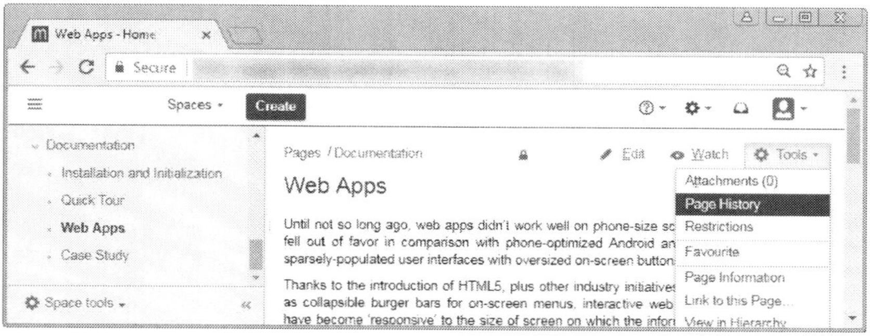

In this professional capacity, I also use online diagramming tools such as Gliffy rather than the erstwhile Microsoft Visio.

This transition to almost exclusively authoring online has completed my conversion to cloud computing. Put simply, I can now use a chromebook rather than a Windows PC even when working with commercial clients.

Working with Web Apps

The ordinary web sites I have just described are web apps in all but name, but not necessarily ones that I 'installed' on my chromebook. You can find additional web apps, and install them (which in most cases is little more than adding shortcuts to them) by visiting the Chrome Web Store.

The Chrome Web Store

Just as the Apple iPad has its iTunes store, and just as Android phones and tablets have the Google Play Store, so Chrome has the Chrome Web Store from where you can install web apps. These web apps, which were originally mostly just packaged web sites rather than locally installable programs, are not necessarily chromebook-specific and in many cases can be used just as effectively when running via the Chrome web browser on your traditional PC.

The Web Store also offers a large number of Chrome browser extensions, which act more like installable utility programs or browser plug-ins. These extensions might perform local tasks - like interacting with your computer hardware - which remotely running web apps cannot perform.

You can visit the Chrome Web Store by clicking the app icon of that name or by typing chrome.google.com/webstore into the Chrome browser's address bar.

Chrome Web Store vs. Google Play Store

This is where is can get a little confusing for first-time chromebook and Chrome users who have used an Android mobile phone or tablet, so let me clarify:

- On a chromebook, you install additional apps from the Chrome Web Store.
- On an Android device, the Google Play Store provides access to additional apps.

So far, so simple, except that the Google Pixelbook and potentially any other chromebook is also an Android device, so you may be able to install the two different kinds of apps from the two app stores. You'll know if you can install an Android app on your chromebook because the Google Play Store will tell you which of your devices are compatible with the Android app you wish to install:

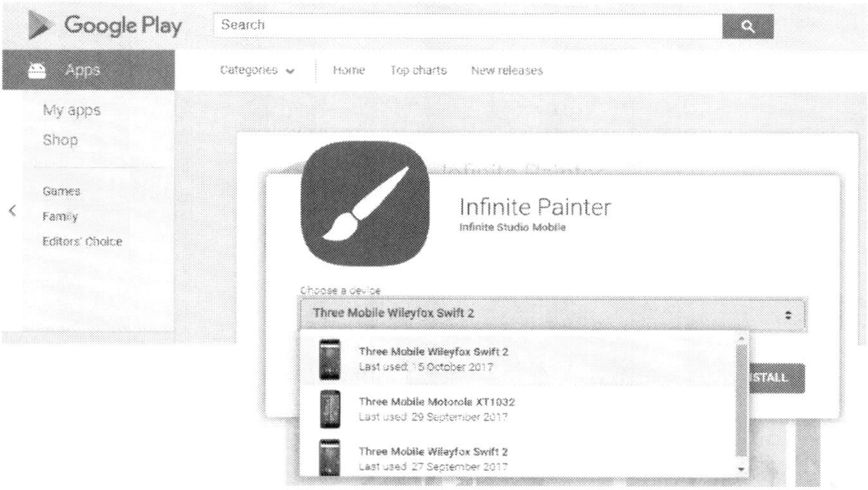

Regardless of what kind of device you're using – chromebook, PC or Android phone / tablet – the Google Play Store is always home to your media content including music, movies and books.

Having taken a temporary detour into the Google Play Store, let's now move back to the Chrome Web Store.

Apps, Extensions and Themes

There are three kinds of things you can install from the Chrome Web Store:

- Apps are rather like the programs you would install on a Windows PC or the apps you would install on an Android device or an iPhone / iPad. The difference is that these Chrome apps are web apps that are not really installed at all, but are merely linked to on the web.
- Extensions are add-ons or plug-ins that are installed into the Chrome browser to provide some functionality across all web apps by extending the capabilities of Chrome itself.
- Themes are a way of styling the look of the browser windows.

In the following picture I have searched the Chrome Web Store for the word "edit" (because I'm interested in editing things) and I have limited my search to apps etc. provided "By Google". You can see how the search results are organized into matching Apps, Extensions and Themes:

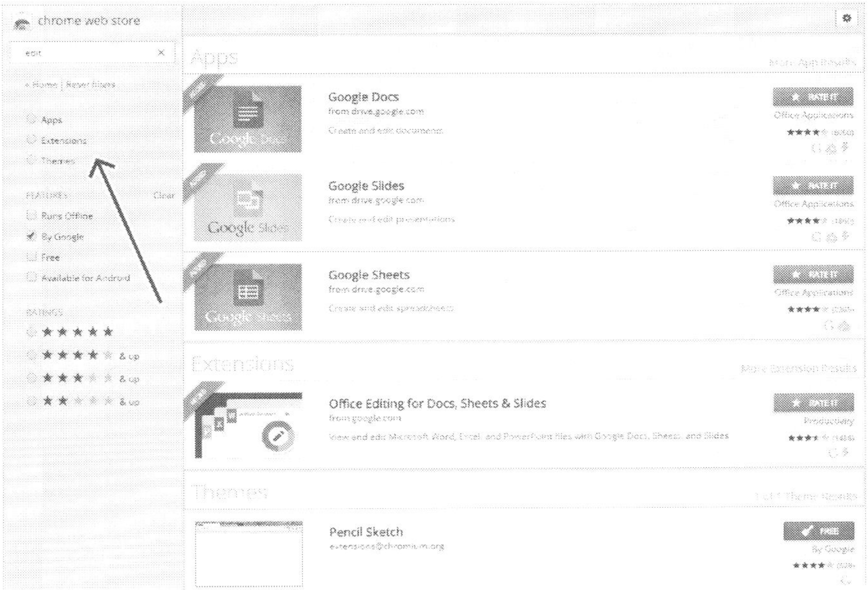

Apps

Any apps you install become available via the Launcher:

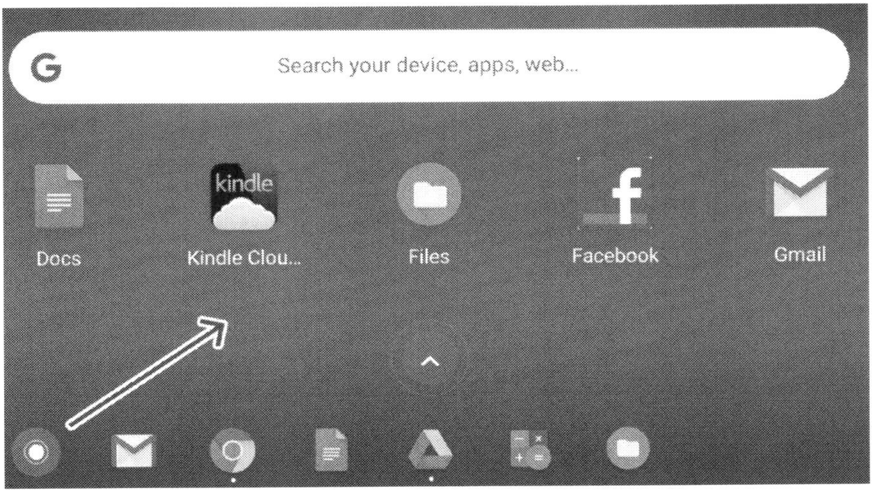

There are actually two kinds of apps in the Chrome Web Store:

- ➢ Websites whereby the 'app' is really just a shortcut to an existing web site. I showed you some of these earlier including QuickBooks Online, Kindle Cloud Reader, and the Pixlr Editor.

➢ "Chrome" apps which may have some HTML, CSS and other content downloaded to your chromebook or PC.

Unlike website apps which are little more than shortcuts to the underlying web sites, Chrome apps have more of their functionality downloaded from the internet to your chromebook or PC. Let's look at one in particular: Google Keep.

Note-taking apps such as Evernote and Microsoft OneNote are quite popular, and Google has its own note-taking app in the form of Google Keep. It allows you to write color-coded notes and lists—the latter allowing you to strike off items as having been completed. Most importantly, these notes are available in your Google Drive at drive.google.com/keep as well as from the Google Keep app itself. Notes can be saved offline (locally on your chromebook or PC) until you are reconnected to the internet, and the notes in the Google Keep app on your Android mobile phone are automatically kept in sync with the Google Keep Chrome app.

In the following picture you can see how the Google Keep app opens in its own window and allows me to take new notes as well as displaying any notes I have already taken; in this case some picture notes:

You might be interested to know that I populated Keep with those particular pictures by copying them from within a Google Docs document, and in this way I am using Keep as a kind of clipboard for my images. This is one of the few ways I have found for getting images out of a Google Docs document for editing; by choosing “Save to Keep notepad” **(1)** then (within the Keep window which opens) right-clicking and choosing “Save picture as...” **(2)**:

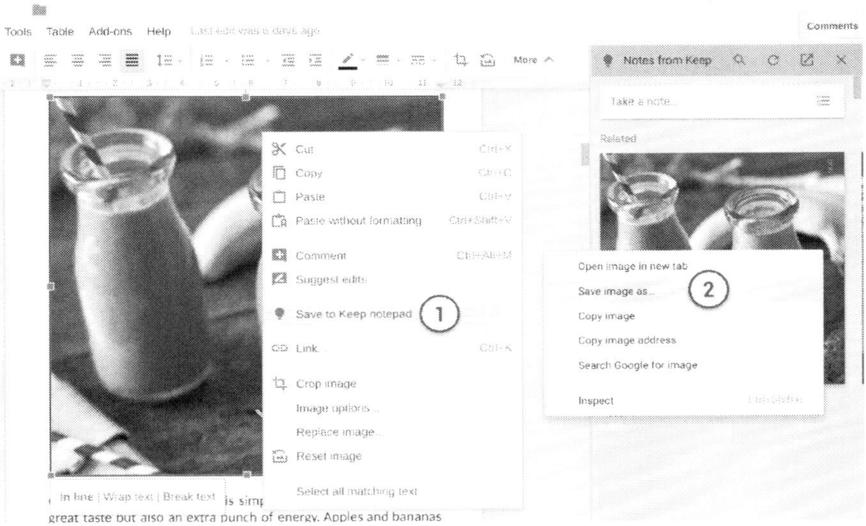

Don’t Forget the Pre-Installed Apps

It’s worth reiterating at this point that when you fire up your chromebook for the first time you will find that several apps are already available via the Apps icons on the app launcher at the bottom of the screen. So when you locate the Google Play Books app (for example) in the Chrome Web Store, you may find that you don’t need to install it at all because it is already installed; and it’s the same story with Google Maps.

Extensions

Chrome extensions are described as small programs that add functionality to your browser, so you can think of them as utilities that do some job regardless of which web site or web app you’re using.

In the following picture you can see the Grammarly extension in action, checking for mistakes I make in an email I am writing. This could be rather important if you regard yourself as a writer like I do.

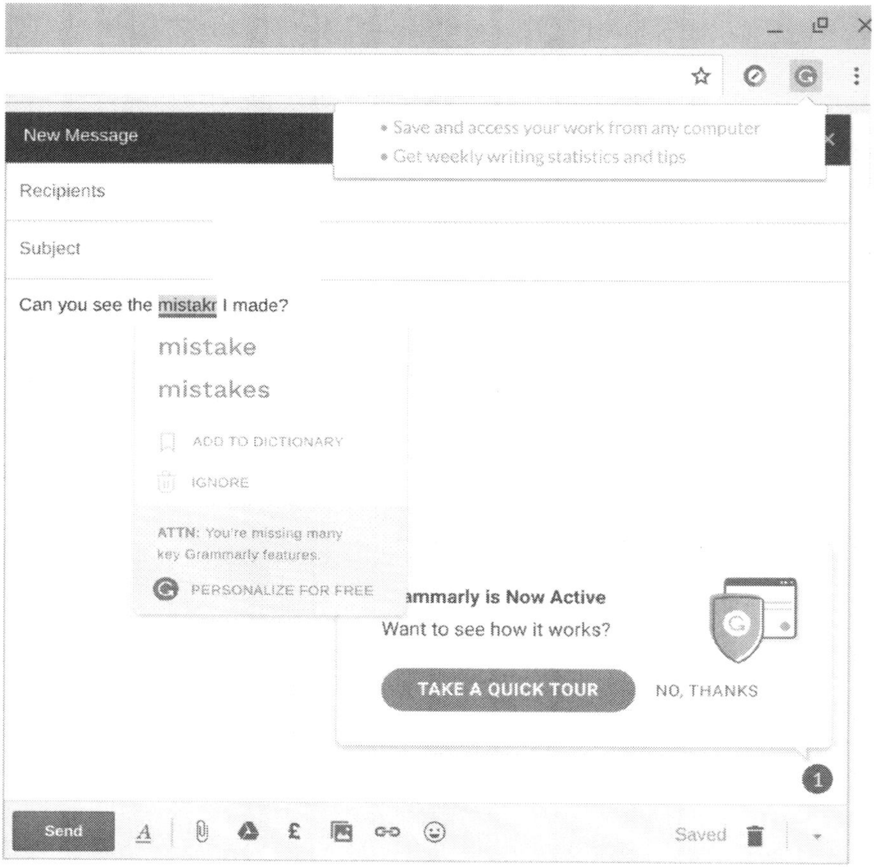

You can see the currently-installed extensions by visiting the web page at chrome://extensions as shown here:

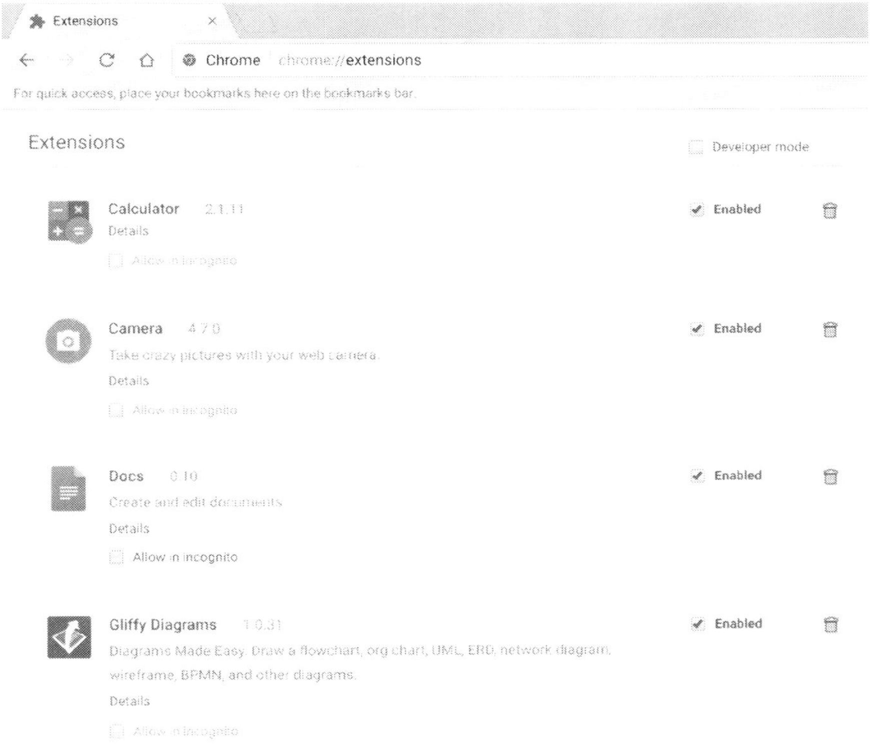

Themes

In addition to apps and extensions, the Chrome Web Store also offers browser Themes. These made perfect sense in the early days when the Chrome web browser occupied the whole of the chromebook screen, but are not so compelling now that chromebooks have a PC-style "desktop" that is unaffected by these in-browser themes and which has its own wallpaper setting. Still, they provide a way to add a little sparkle to your browsing session—for example by installing the metallic "Brushed" theme as shown above.

Chapter Summary

In the first part of this chapter I introduced the Chrome web browser which is the centerpiece of Google's cloud computing experience. I told you how you can open web pages in new browser windows or in tabs within an existing browser window, and I introduced the omnibox via which you can search the web as well as enter a direct web address. I introduced some other browser features (and settings) and I explained how signing into Chrome - which is implicit when using a chromebook - allows you to take your browsing experience (web history, etc.) from device to device.

In the second part of this chapter I introduced you to web apps, which are basically just very interactive web sites that are made more accessible via installed application shortcuts. I presented the Chrome Web Store (which is home to Chrome web apps, extensions and themes) as distinct from the Google Play Store (which is home to Android apps plus media content such as movies, music, and books).

About Android Apps

The Google Pixelbook in particular, and up-and-coming chromebooks in general, offer support for Android apps as well as Chrome OS web apps. This could be the game changer Google needs in order to make chromebooks more mainstream computer choices, for three principal reasons:

➢ Android apps are more like traditional apps or programs that you install on your computer, and which – in many cases – can be run when disconnected from the internet.

➢ Android apps are obtainable from an extensive established app store – the Google Play Store – which offers many apps that do not (yet) have web app equivalents.

➢ Many users of Android phones and tablets are already familiar with, and invested in, their favorite Android apps.

Installing Android Apps

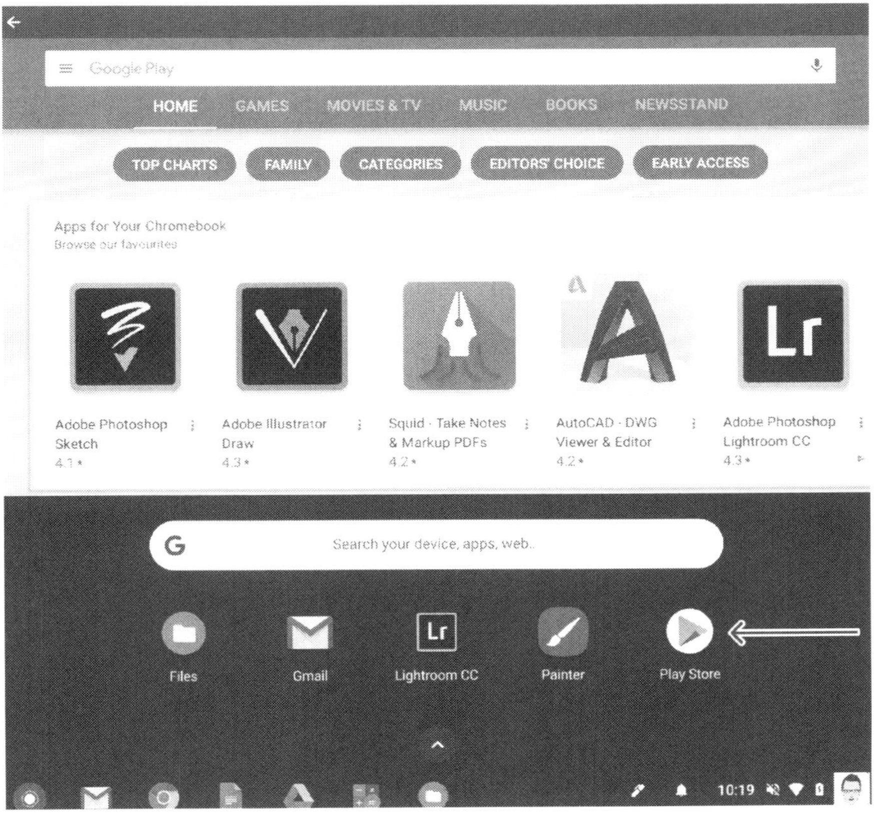

Unlike web apps which are installed from the Chrome Web Store (if at all, because they're mostly just websites), Android apps are installed from the Google Play store in exactly the same way as with your Android phone.

One of the ways in which Android apps differ from web apps is in the fact that you may periodically be prompted to update them, whereas with web apps you are always accessing the latest online versions: no re-installation required.

One concern about installing Android apps on a chromebook may be security, especially since the original idea of cloud computing with chromebooks was to have few (if any) user-installed programs. To allay this concern, I understand that Android apps run in their own walled garden or 'sandbox', separate from the main Chrome OS, so that security issues are at least minimized.

Scaling Up the Screen

Whereas Android apps may appear initially in their smaller mobile phone orientations, they can be dynamically resized to fill more of the screen, and you can move them around the desktop like any other windows. The following picture shows the Adobe Lightroom Android app in its original orientation next to the Infinite Painter Android app that has been resized:

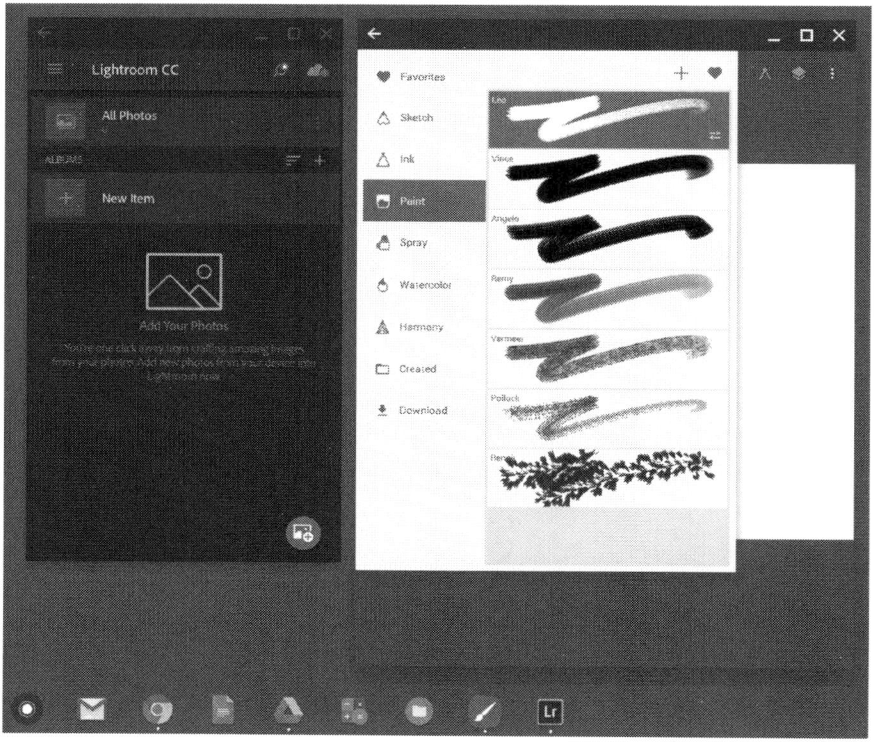

You can also maximize any Android app to fill the full screen, and indeed this will happen automatically (i.e. you can only see one Android app at a time) when the Pixelbook screen is flipped over to its tablet form factor. Not to worry, you can easily switch between your Android apps and other windows by tapping the **switch windows** key or on-screen button:

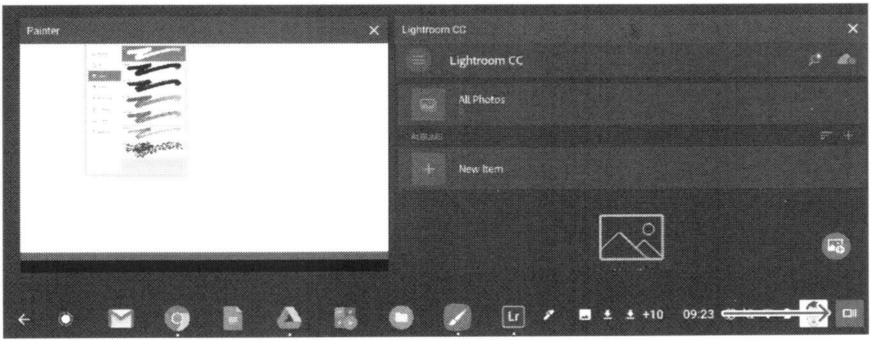

Microsoft Office Android Apps

As a professional writer, one of the biggest bugbears I might have had about the original chromebook concept was the lack of support for Microsoft Office apps such as Word. This is not the problem that it used to be now that Google Docs has matured to the level at which writing a book like this one is possible, and likewise for Microsoft Word Online, but for some of you there may still be some very good reasons for working with Word documents entirely offline. This is possible via the Microsoft Office Android apps (see below) which you may already have made use of on your mobile phone or Android tablet.

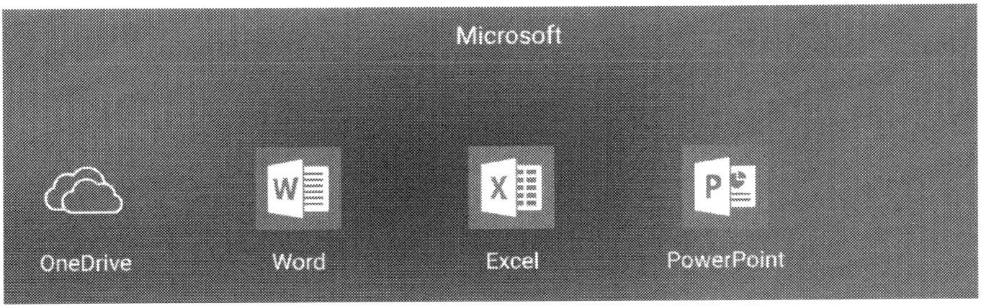

These apps might not do absolutely everything their Windows desktop equivalents do, but at least they provide a third way of work of working with Office files, so now you can work with Microsoft Office files using:

- Google Docs / Drive.
- Microsoft Office Online / OneDrive.
- Office Android apps.

As you can see in the following picture, the Android app for Microsoft Word provides a very credible document editing experience including support for advanced features such as "track changes". And the same goes for the Excel app.

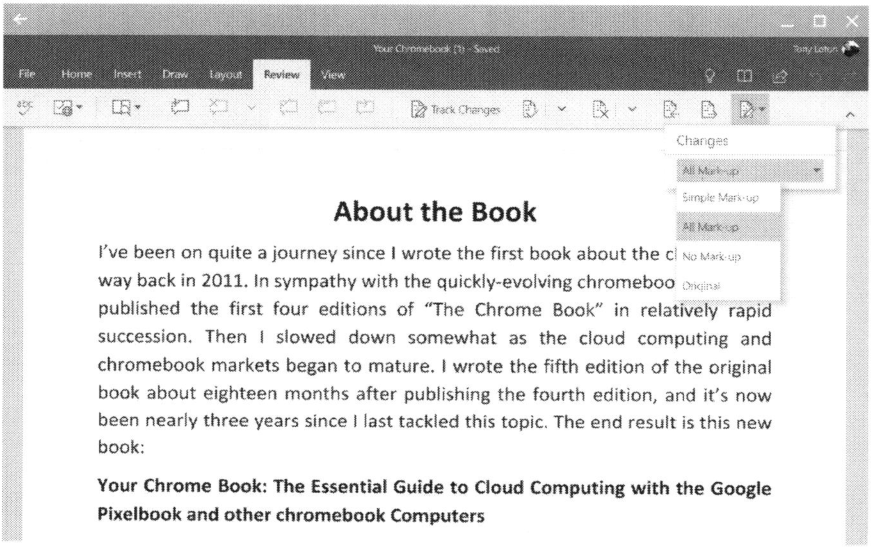

Web Apps and Their Android Alternatives

Since chromebooks now support Android apps, in many cases there is now more than one way to do exactly the same thing. For any given task, you now typically have a choice between the web app and its equivalent Android app.

Want to communicate using Skype? You can now choose between the "Skype for Web" app available from the Chrome Web Store, or the Skype Android app available from the Google Play Store. The same thing goes for Facebook and many other applications; not limited only to social networking.

These two kinds of apps are not always exactly equivalent, and which one you choose may depend on exactly what you want to do. As a concrete example: whereas the Kindle Cloud Reader web app (first picture below) lets me perform a certain set of functions on selected text, the Kindle Android app (second picture below) allows me – for example – to COPY text in a way that the web app can't. This may be important to me when wanting to convert one of my clients' existing Kindle books into a print book manuscript.

Anecdotally, I have also found a use for the Android app version of the Chrome web browser on my chromebook, even though it already has the native Chrome web browser already built in:

When trying to access my bank's investment web site, I was somewhat shocked to see the message that my chromebook's up-to-date Chrome browser was not new enough to display their interactive investment platform. This apparent problem was solved simply by installing the Chrome browser Android app and accessing the problematic website through it instead.

Taking this idea still further, there is now no need for you to be dependent on the Chrome web browser at all. Here are a few of the others that I installed on my Pixelbook as Android apps:

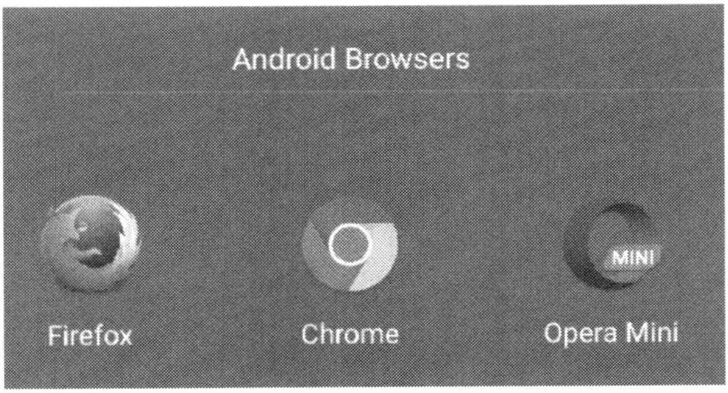

Having just told you how Android apps may have the edge over web apps in some situations, I'm now going to tell you why we may soon not need Android apps at all.

No Need for Android Apps At All?

When Google first came up with the concept of Chrome OS and the chromebooks, they seemed to be envisioning a world in which the web browser (specifically Chrome) would be at the center of everyone's world with one-size-fits-all web apps running on any device that had a web browser. This initiative was somewhat undermined by the popularity of iPhone- and Android-specific app stores that took us back to the days when programs were produced for specific device operating systems. And it's one of the reasons that chromebooks took a while to gain traction outside of academic environments.

Although chromebooks now support Android apps, this may not actually be necessary, and it may be possible for Google to yet to achieve its original aim of having users interacting only with their web browsers. This is thanks responsive web apps that run just as well in the browser on an Android phone as they do on chromebooks and other personal computers.

About Responsive Web Apps

Until not so long ago, web apps didn't work well on phone-size screens, so such web apps fell out of favor in comparison with phone-optimized Android and iOS apps that sported sparsely-populated user interfaces with oversized on-screen buttons for fat fingers.

Thanks to the introduction of HTML5, plus other industry initiatives and best practices such as collapsible burger bars for on-screen menus, interactive web sites for everyday tasks have become 'responsive' to the size of screen on which the information is to be displayed. Consider the BBC News website that automatically adjusts the size and shape of its content according to the size of the web browser window.

Thanks to this kind of adaptive display of information, you would see the more detailed widescreen version when viewing in a web browser on a big screen, and you would see the scaled down portrait presentation when seeing the exact same content on a phone screen. Thus there may no longer be any need for a phone-optimized app for BBC News content because one website fits all devices. *See the first picture(s) that follow.*

Taking this a stage further, some organizations offer separate mobile versions of their web sites. In some case these mobile-optimized web apps now offer equivalent functionality that is presented in a similar way to the equivalent Android apps. One specific case that comes to mind is the QuickBooks online mobile-optimized web site. *See the second picture(s) that follow.*

Have Your Say - BBC News
BBC
Home
News
More
NEWS
Have Your Say
How to share with BBC News
Have you got a good story? BBC News would like to hear from you. Email us haveyoursay@bbc.co.uk Get in touch via SMS 61124 Or contact us via WhatsApp
9 February 2017 Have Your Say
What do you want the BBC to investigate?
Contact us on WhatsApp
What do you want us to investigate?

Have Your Say - BBC News
BBC
Home
News
Sport
Weather
iPlayer
More
NEWS
Have Your Say
How to share with BBC News
What do you want the BBC to investigate?
Contact us on WhatsApp
Ask us anything...
0:19
What do you want us to investigate?
Brexit: What are your views?

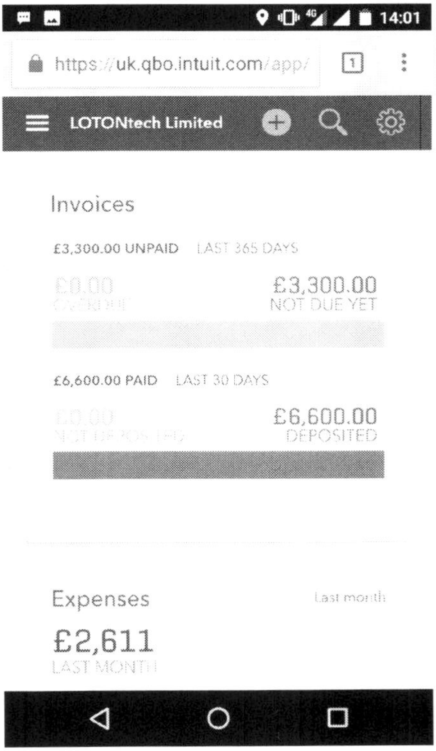
14:01
https://uk.qbo.intuit.com/app/
LOTONtech Limited
Invoices
£3,300.00 UNPAID LAST 365 DAYS
£3,300.00
NOT DUE YET
£6,600.00 PAID LAST 30 DAYS
£6,600.00
DEPOSITED
Expenses
Last month
£2,611
LAST MONTH

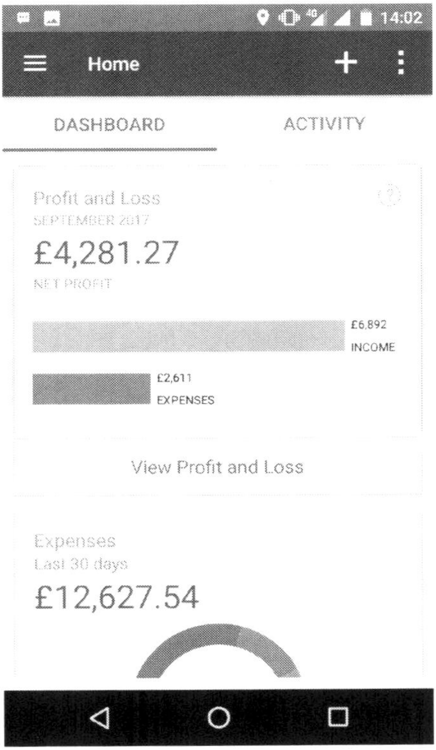
14:02
Home
DASHBOARD
ACTIVITY
Profit and Loss
SEPTEMBER 2017
£4,281.27
NET PROFIT
£6,892
INCOME
£2,611
EXPENSES
View Profit and Loss
Expenses
Last 30 days
£12,627.54

The upshot to all this is that whereas Android apps possibly still rule the roost in terms of phone-optimized functionality, and therefore it's a good thing that Chrome OS supports them, the alternative of one-size-fits-all web apps may well be gaining ground.

Chapter Summary

In this chapter I have explained how you can install Android apps from the Google Play Store onto your chromebook.

I have introduced the Microsoft Office Android apps, and have further explained how for every web app there is probably an alternative Android app (and vice versa). This led me to my speculation that - while useful as a functional stop-gap on chromebooks - we may eventually not need Android apps at all, which would complete the realization of Google's original vision for cloud computing with chromebooks.

In an interesting juxtaposition, the chromebook-cum-Android tablet has already existed for some time before Chrome OS support for Android apps, for the simple reason that Android tablets run the Chrome web browser which provides access to the exactly the same web apps as Chrome OS itself.

Your Google Account(s)

When you first set up your chromebook, you had to sign in to an existing Google Account or create a new one. *You can also "sign in" to the Chrome web browser on your Windows PC or other device, so that certain elements of your experience are shared across devices.*

Whenever you power up the chromebook in future - and assuming other family members, friends or work colleagues have used your chromebook (which is all part of the plan) - then you will be presented with a sign-in screen that allows you to choose which identity to log in as; or to add a new user for one of the aforementioned friends, family, or colleagues.

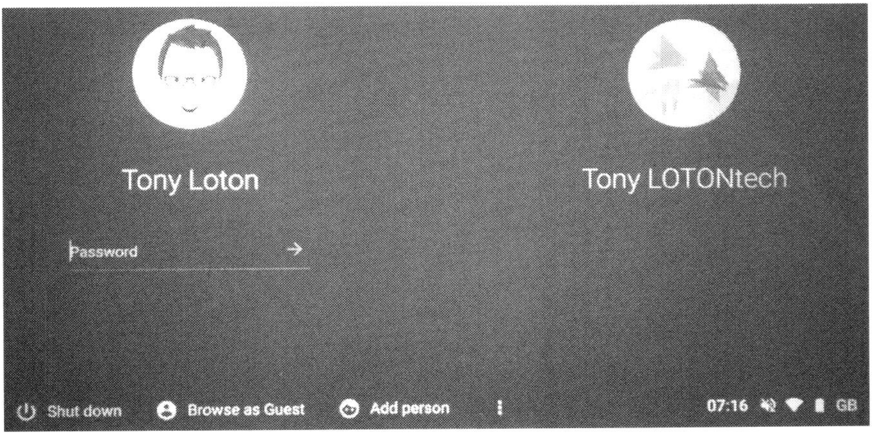

Note that the Google Account that you log in with during the initial setup will become the master account or "owner" account that can manage all other users.

Sign-In Synchronization

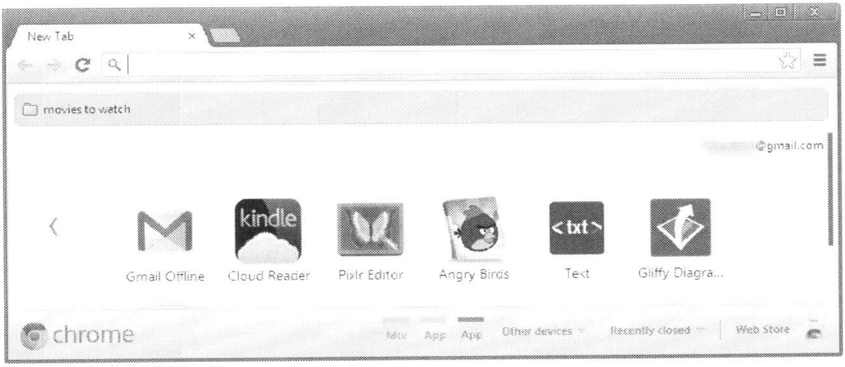

As an example in earlier editions of this book, on my chromebook I created a set of bookmarks in a folder named "movies to watch". I installed some apps from the Chrome Web Store, and upon launching the Chrome web browser on my PC I was presented with exactly the same bookmarks and choice of apps as shown above.

It's your central Google Account that makes this cross-device synchronization possible, and it's your Google Account that allows you to use other features such as Google Cloud Print and the Chrome Remote Desktop which are both explained in a later chapter.

Your Google Account is also the common thread that runs through your Gmail, Google Drive, Blogger and other Google services.

You can manage your Google account by visiting the web page at myaccount.google.com or by choosing the "My Account" link from the pull-down menu of options available when you click your email address at the top-right of your browser pages when using any Google application:

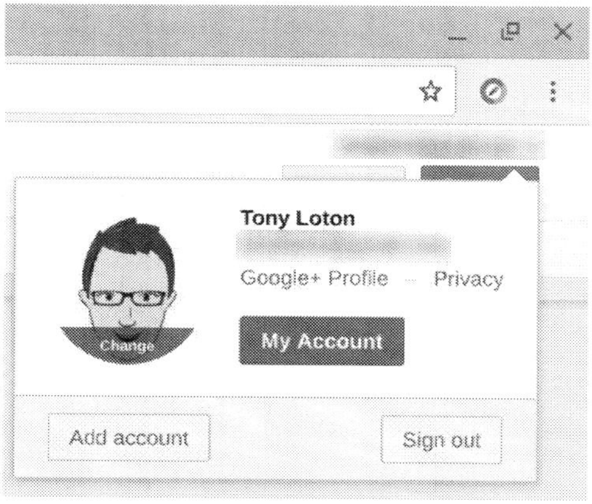

There are various things you can manage on an account, depending on whether it is a personal account or a company (staff) account set up for you by an organization via Google Apps. Two of the most important things you will want to manage are your cloud storage and your security. So now let's look at those.

Cloud Storage

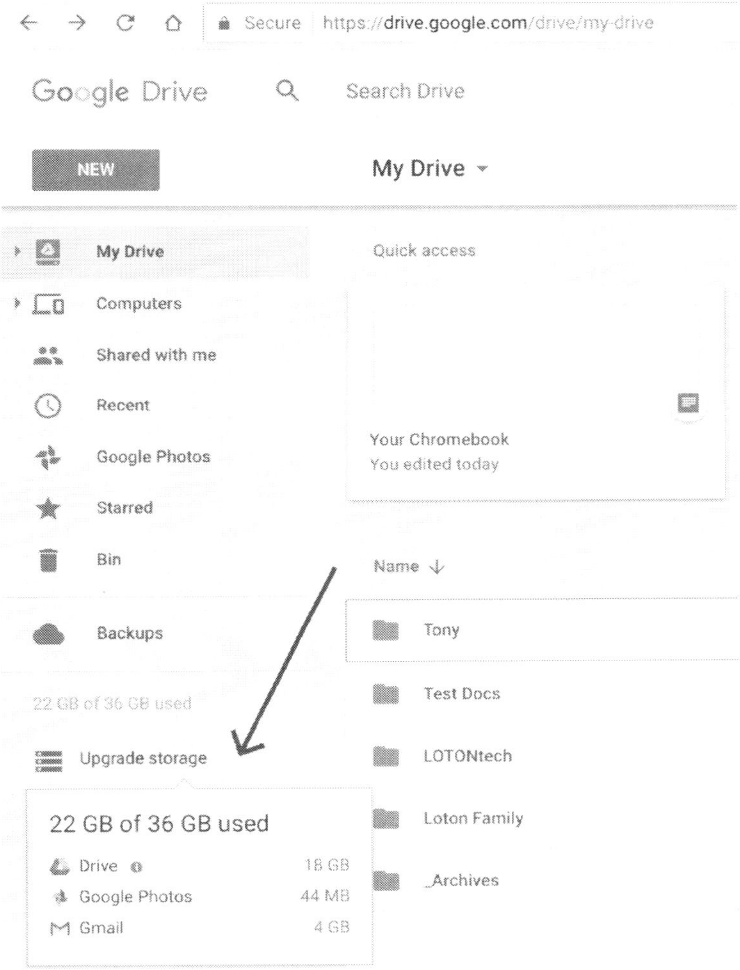

Besides being able to access your available cloud storage and settings from the My Account page, you can also see and upgrade your storage via the Google Drive web page as shown above.

Everyone is given a certain amount of free storage with their Google Account, in addition to which:

- Google sometimes runs promotions where it offers additional storage (for example) to purchasers of Google devices.
- You can purchase additional storage on an annual or monthly plan.

In the following picture you can see how my current Drive storage is made up of a combination of a paid plan (20 GB), an early adopter bonus (1 GB) and a paid user bonus (15 GB):

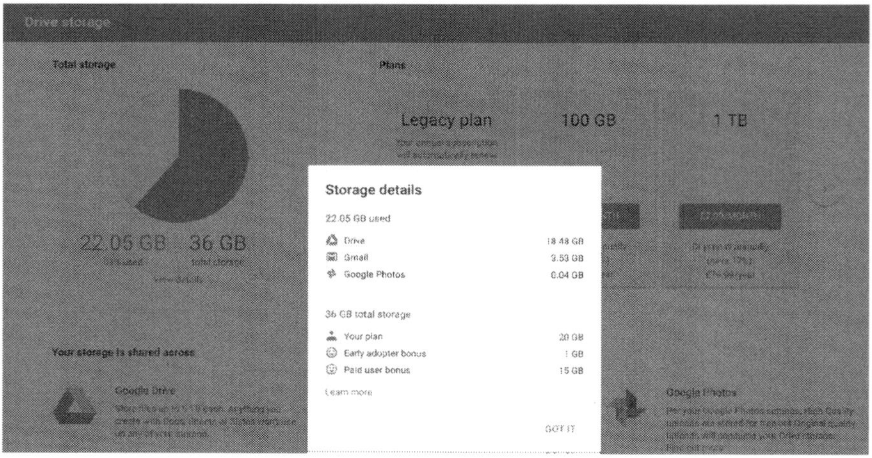

Note that while uploaded non-Google files eat away at your cloud storage, your Google Docs, Sheets and Slides won't count against your allowance. This is great news for me now that I have almost entirely ditched Microsoft Office in order to work almost wholly with Google Docs.

Security

The most important thing you will do in your Google Account is to manage your password. Since your Gmail address and password combination is the key to everything stored in your Google cloud, it is important that you remember it while at the same time not making it obvious and guessable.

Fortunately, you are provided with a couple of mechanisms for recovering your password in the event that you forget what it is. You can record an alternative recovery email address to which a password reminder can be sent, and you can specify a security question such as "What is the name of your best friend from childhood?" which you will be asked in the event that you wish to reset your password.

Note that if ever you change your Google password - which arguably you should do periodically - you will have to update any client devices that sign into your Google account. For example, the Gmail application on your Android mobile phone will prompt you for your password when it finds that a connection cannot be made using your old password.

Multiple Google Accounts

I like to have at least two Google accounts, mainly so that I have separate business and personal email addresses. Therefore, I sometimes need to log into two different accounts simultaneously on the same chromebook or another device. There are several ways to achieve this, some of which are more effective than others, and only one of which reduces the possibility of confusion down to zero.

Add Person (on the login screen)

Chromebooks, Windows PCs, and most if not all computers these days allow multiple users to sign into a single computer using different identities... and to switch between these user identities with just a few keystrokes. This is the best approach for almost eliminating the possibility of working with the wrong account if you have more than one.

On a chromebook it is possible to sign in to the computer via various user identities (Google Accounts) and it takes seconds to switch between them via the chromebook sign-in screen; reminder below.

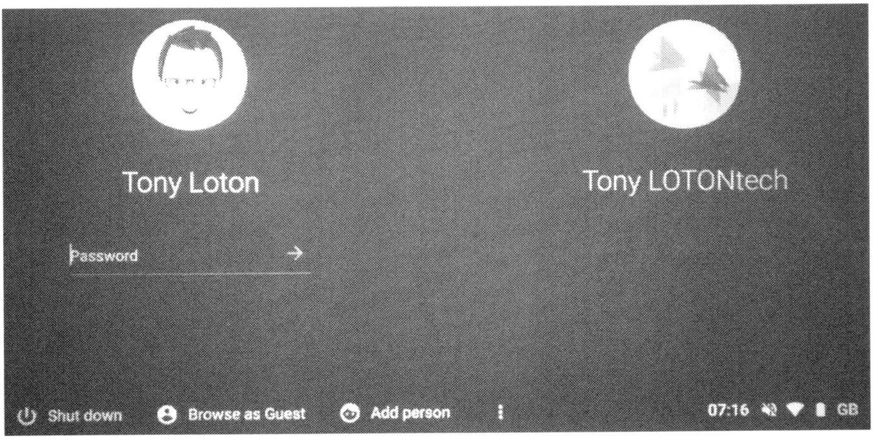

You can see my two login accounts in this picture, with the second one having been added to the login screen by clicking the "Add persion" link at the bottom of the screen.

To switch from one identity to another via this screen, click your profile picture at the bottom-right of the chromebook screen and choose "Sign out".

Different Browsers

When cloud computing on a Windows PC that runs different brands of web browser, my preference is to assume different identities (sign into different

Google accounts) in different web browsers: e.g. the Chrome web browser for my personal Gmail, and the Mozilla Firefox web browser for my business Gmail.

This wasn't so easy to achieve on a chromebook that only ran the Chrome web browser, but the more recent support for Android apps raises the possibility of running other web browsers on a chromebook in the Android incarnations. I have even run the chromebook's native Chrome browser and the Chrome browser Android app side-by-side to access my personal and business emails at the same time.

Different Email Identities

Since my main reason for having two different Google Accounts is to use two different email addresses, I can actually solve the same problem in an entirely different way by:

- ➢ Configuring my business email to automatically forward messages to my personal email address (first picture below).
- ➢ Configuring my personal Gmail account to be able to "Send mail as:" different email identities (second picture below).

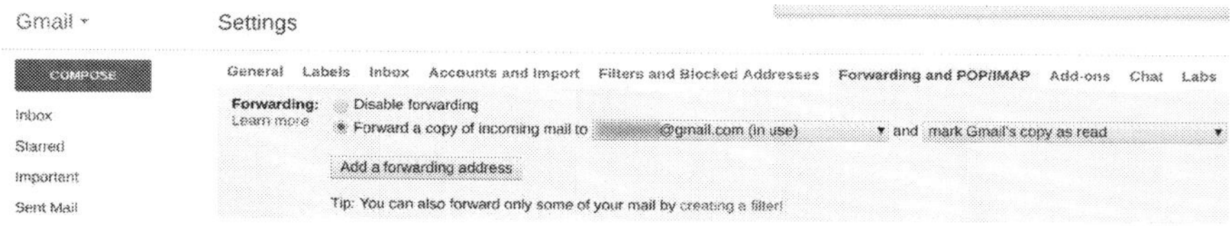

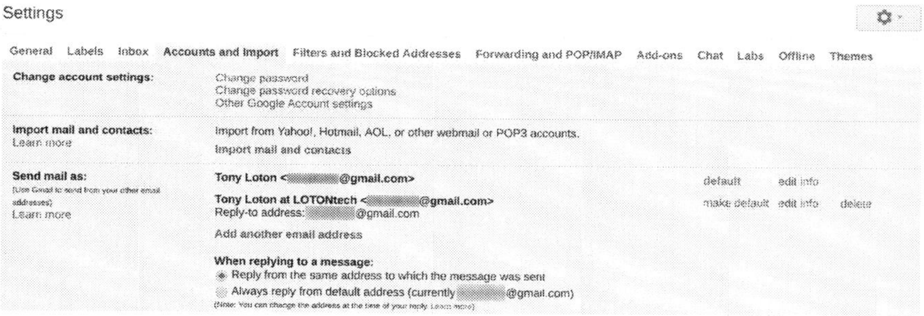

The upshot to all this is that I receive all my incoming personal and business email in my personal Inbox, and I can send email from either email address from within my personal Gmail:

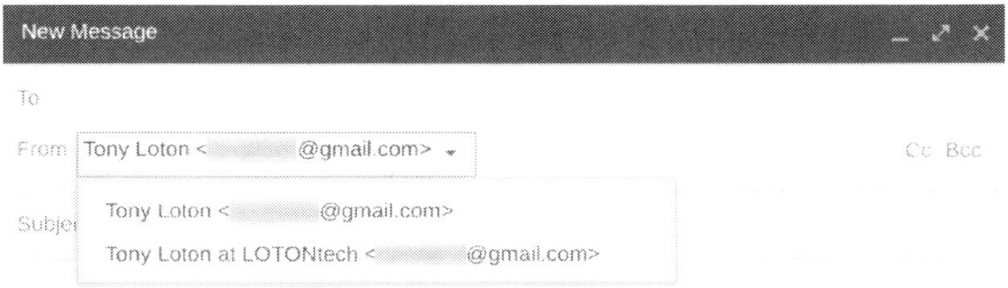

Restricting Chromebook User Accounts

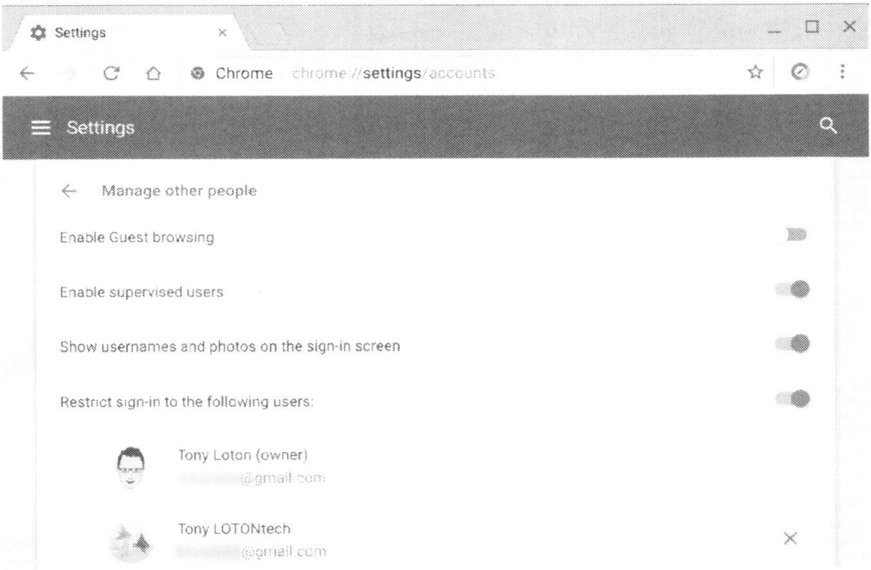

Unless you expressly forbid it, anyone with a Google Account can sign in to your chromebook. It's nothing to worry about, and is all part of the plan, because the whole point is that (theoretically, at least) anyone can access their Google account, apps and settings via any Chrome device anywhere. Which includes you, if you happen to lose your chromebook or its gets damaged, in which case you can get up-and-running again really quickly by finding a friend with a chromebook or by going out and buying another one. It's not like the old days when, if you lost or damaged your PC, you'd have lost all of the files and programs stored on it.

If you do want to restrict the users who can log into your chromebook, or if you want to disable the guest browsing feature, you can do so by clicking the

"Manage other users" button on the Settings web page at chrome://settings/accounts as shown above.

Chapter Summary

In this chapter I described how your Google Account is your key into the world of cloud computing with Chrome.

After mentioning account security and cloud storage, I addressed the issue of multiple user accounts in two contexts: if you have more than one Google account (perhaps for business and pleasure) and if you want (or don't want) other Google account users to sign into your chromebook.

Email, Calendar and Communication

One of the main things people use their computers for is to communicate with other people; via email (obviously) but less-obviously via calendar (by inviting people to events or simply communicating your availability for events). We can also include instant messaging, voice and video calling using services such as Skype, Google Hangouts and social networks such as Facebook.

Gmail

When you're cloud computing with Chrome on a chromebook, email will most likely mean Gmail. It doesn't have to, since other email providers such as Yahoo! and Microsoft Outlook have web interfaces that you can use just as well via the Chrome browser. But you will probably migrate to Gmail in the end because the Google Account associated with your Gmail email address will be your handle for logging into your chromebook, the Chrome web browser, and Google's cloud computing services.

You can access Gmail by launching the Gmail app or by simply typing mail.google.com into the Chrome browser address bar.

I won't be offering a start-from-scratch email tutorial here since most if not all of you will already be familiar with using an email interface, so I'll concentrate of a few topics that will help you adjust to Gmail if you've been using another email provider.

Migrating to Gmail

If you're not already using Gmail, the chances are good that you're using another web-based email provider like Yahoo! Mail or Hotmail. While it is possible to continue using these providers (and there is even a Yahoo! Mail app for Chrome) you might like to consider migrating to Gmail so that Google becomes your one-stop-shop with a single sign-in for email, calendar (discussed next) and documents on your PC, chromebook and Android mobile phone. If you like the sound of this idea, you'll need some help with migrating to Gmail.

Note that if you don't already have an email address with another provider, you can safely skip ahead to the next section about labelling Gmail messages without worrying about migrating your email at all.

If you have a chromebook or Android phone, you will already have Google Account that you use to log in, therefore you will most likely already have a Gmail address of the form yourgoogleaccountname@gmail.com. What you won't yet have is access to the messages still flowing into your old email address; the messages you will want to see until you have notified all of your contacts that you have changed your email address to a Gmail one. So let's look at channeling messages from your old email address through to the Gmail interface.

You don't have to do this, because you could simply keep logging into your old email account to check for new messages—for example by typing mail.live.com into the Chrome web browser's omnibox to access your Microsoft Hotmail account. But I think it helps with the transition to cloud computing with Chrome if you move decisively to Gmail as your single email application.

There are two ways in which you can channel incoming email messages from your old provider to Gmail. The first way is to forward the incoming messages, which I can demonstrate using the Yahoo! Mail POP & Forwarding options shown below.

Notice that I have checked the option to "Forward your (BT) Yahoo! Mail" and I have entered my new Gmail email address. Also note that this setting is at the Yahoo! end rather than at the Gmail end.

The forwarding technique allows your old email provider to push incoming messages into your Gmail account. The other technique is for Gmail to pull the incoming messages from your old account, the key to which is also contained in the figure above. Notice how I could have checked the option to "Allow your (BT) Yahoo! Mail to be POPped" instead, in which case I would also need to do something in my Gmail account so as to actually do the POPping.

Clicking the small cog wheel at the top-right of your Gmail screen displays a pull-down menu from which you can select the option to adjust your mail Settings. On the settings page you can select the "Accounts and Import" tab in order to set up one or more Post Office Protocol (POP) accounts within the "Check email from other accounts" section of the page:

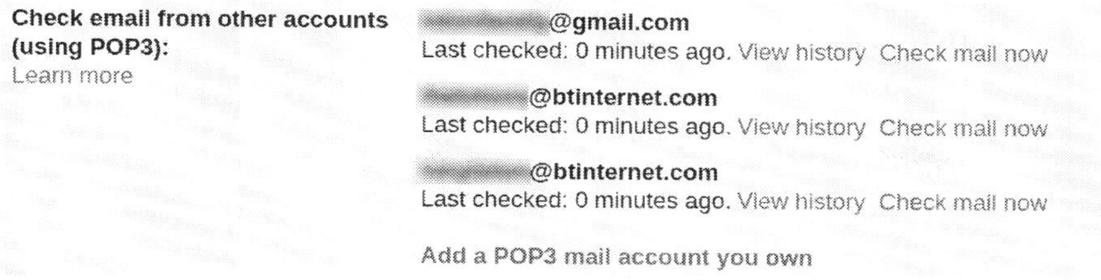

You can see that the 'old' email accounts I have set up for POPing are checked periodically, and you can set up a new legacy account by clicking the link labeled "Add a POP3 mail account you own". You will be guided through the setup process which will ask for your old email address (from which the correct settings will be determined automatically) and will send an email to your old email address containing a verification code that you will need to enter in order to complete the process. In case you haven't figured it out, the verification step is to ensure that you really do own the old email account and that you are not fetching someone else's private correspondence into your Inbox.

On the subject of your Inbox; this is where any new emails to your old email address will now appear unless you decide to 'label' them as part of the setup process. This brings us nicely to the concept of labeling your email messages.

Labeling Gmail Messages

The Inbox is home to your incoming email messages, but many web-based email providers allow you to move messages from your Inbox into specific folders. Gmail allows you to do a similar thing by labeling your messages as shown below. You can see in this example how I have applied the Personal and Work labels to three of the messages in my Inbox using the Labels drop-down menu. You can also see how I could create new labels and manage labels.

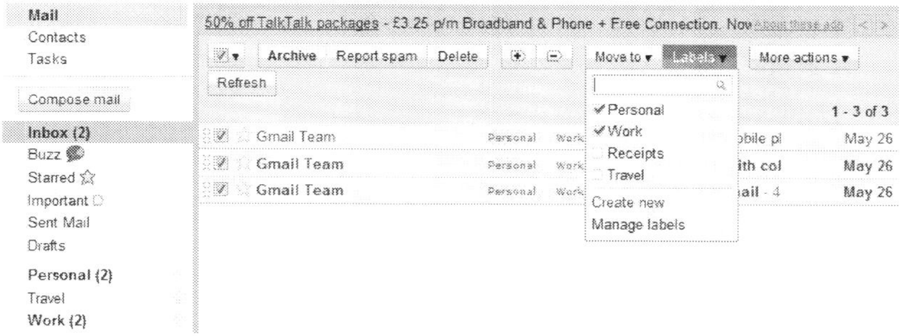

Note that in more recent versions of Gmail, the pull-down list of headings for "Move to" and "Labels" has been replaced by icons, but I have used the version with textual list headings for clarity.

It is possible to nest labels within labels so as to create a hierarchy (how about "Personal / 2013" and "Personal / 2014" and so on?) and you should have figured out from my example that any message can be given more than one label. By selecting the Personal label (in the far left column) I will be able to filter all messages labeled Personal regardless of which other labels are applied to those messages.

So, you can label your messages, but they will still clog up your Inbox, won't they? You can move them out of the Inbox using the "Move to" drop-down menu that you can see in the above figure. Although the effect is similar to moving a message to a new or existing label, I think this particular option might be better named "Move from", because it disconnects the message from whichever labeled folder you are viewing and moves it to the new or existing label while retaining all other labels. So in my example, the effect of moving my already-labeled messages to the Travel label would be to remove the Inbox label while retaining the existing Personal and Work labels in addition to the new Travel label. So in a sense, I moved this message *from the Inbox* rather than *to Travel.*

Composing Gmail Messages with Google Drive Attachments

Although it wasn't always the case, it is now possible to attach a Google Drive file directly to an email message rather than having to download it to your Downloads folder first. In the email composition window click the Drive icon **(1)**, then choose whether to insert as a link **(2)** or an attachment **(3)** before actually doing the insert **(4)**:

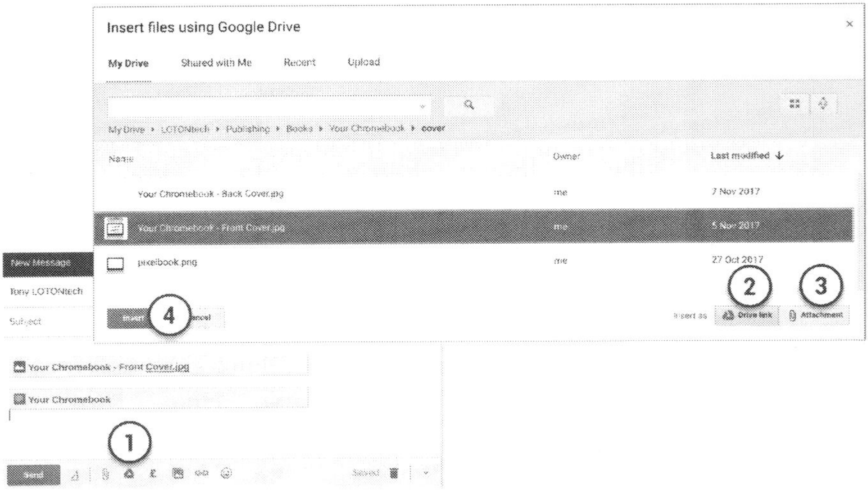

For non-Google files such as a JPEG image you have the option of sending the file as a link or an attachment, with the former being of greatest benefit if the file is too big to be sent as an attachment. For Google files such as Docs, Sheets and Slides the attachment option will be unavailable and you will always email a link.

Using Gmail Offline

As a further step towards making chromebooks useable when not connected to the internet, Google offers a Gmail Offline application that is available in the Chrome Web Store. Although this app runs within a browser window, it provides a user interface not unlike traditional email clients like Microsoft Outlook with the ability to read and compose messages when no internet connection is available.

Contacts, Calling and Chat

Readers under a certain age might not even know what I'm talking about next, but...

Not so many years ago, weren't you just sick of typing all your contacts into your mobile phone and then having to retype them when you changed phones? For the more technical readers: weren't you sick of syncing the contacts between your web-mail provider, the email application (such as Outlook) on your PC, and your mobile phone, only to find that some contacts had gone missing during the move or had their 'home' and 'mobile' numbers mysteriously switched around?

Let's keep it really simple then, by using your Google Contacts list as the central repository for all your contacts. Watch how they magically get synced with the People or Contacts app on your Android mobile phone... and never get lost.

You can access your Gmail contact list by clicking the Gmail pull-down at the top-left of your Gmail session, and then clicking the Contacts item as shown below:

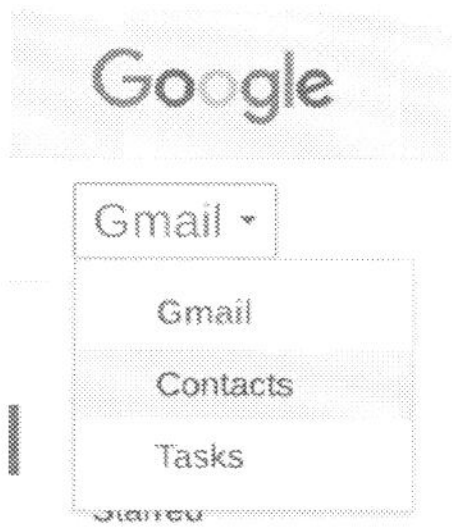

The reason you have those contacts is, of course, so that you can contact them... and not just by email. Skype users will be well versed in contacting their contacts via instant messages, voice calls, and video calls. You can do the same things from within Gmail via a Hangout.

Google Hangouts

Hangouts is Google's answer to Facebook Messenger or Microsoft's Skype: a one-stop-shop for communicating with one or more friends or colleagues via instant messages or video calls.

At the bottom-left of the Gmail screen you can click the "+" icon next to your name **(1)**, search for and choose a correspondent contact **(2)**, and engage them in conversation **(3)** as well as optionally starting a video call **(4)**:

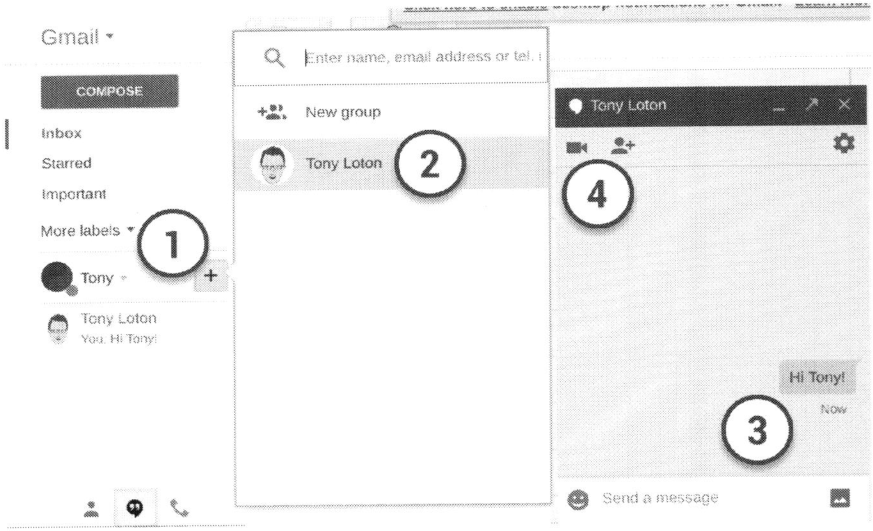

At the other end of the Hangouts connection, your correspondent can respond with text or initiate a video call.

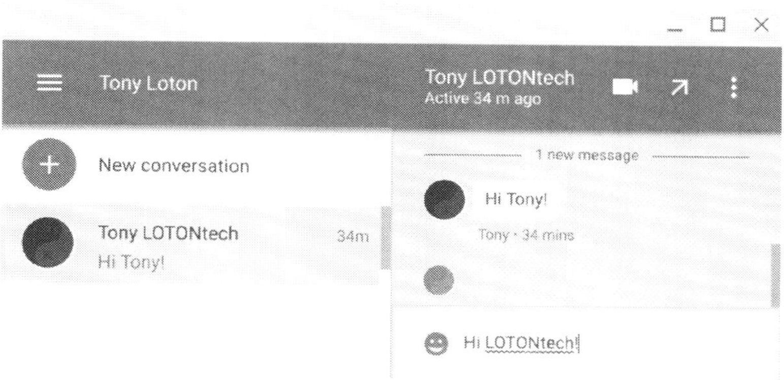

Note that as well as being able to initiate a Hangouts conversation from within the Gmail interface, your chromebook also has a dedicated Hangouts app, which is what you can see in the previous picture. The same app is available on Android phones.

Google Calendar

All good personal information management (PIM) software such as Microsoft Outlook, every good web-based email provider, and all good mobile phone operating systems offer a calendar application to complement the email and contacts applications. Google Calendar provides all the calendar functionality you are likely to need. You can set up multiple calendars—maybe one for business, and one for personal appointments. You can invite your friends or colleagues to events that you schedule in your calendar, and you can even access your friends' calendars (if they let you). You can view calendars by day, week, or month, and you can subscribe to calendar feeds from other calendars such as the UK Holidays calendar feed as shown below.

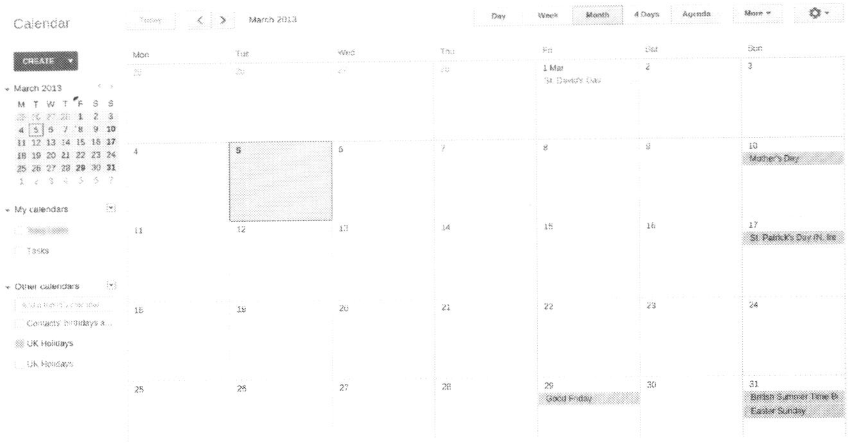

If you're migrating to Google Calendar from another calendar application, you will be pleased to know that you won't have to retype all of your existing entries. Just click the "Other calendars" link that you can see at the bottom-left of the previous picture, choose "Import calendar", and browse for an iCal or CSV file that you have exported from Microsoft Outlook, Yahoo! Calendar, or whichever calendar application you used previously.

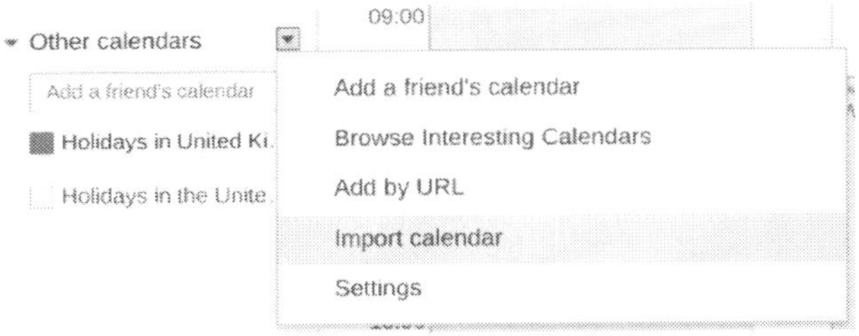

Don't forget that because the Google Calendar is entirely web-based, you can access your calendar from any computer anywhere as long as it has a web browser.

Using Google Calendar Offline

Just as you can access your Gmail email offline when disconnected from the internet, so you can also access your Google Calendar offline. Simply click the cogwheel / gear icon at the top-right of the calendar **(1)** and select the Offline option **(2)**, then heed the warning about offline access on shared computers **(3)**.

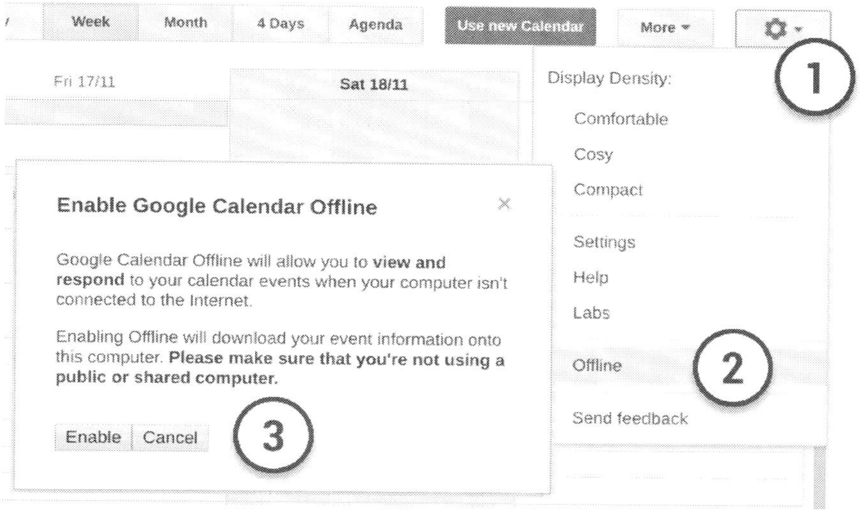

Synchronized with Android

One of the most useful features of the Google mail, contacts and calendar suite is that it synchronizes automatically with those same apps on your Android mobile phone, providing you use the same Google Account on each device. Enter a new contact or calendar entry via your PC, chromebook, or Android phone and see it synced automatically on all the other devices. Gone are the days when you had to do a three-way-sync between your mobile phone, Microsoft Outlook running on your PC, and your online email or calendar provided by Yahoo! or Google—so no more important meetings or contacts need go astray.

Chapter Summary

In this chapter I have introduced a subset of Chrome apps that support social activities; i.e. interacting with other people via email, chats and video calls, and scheduled meetings via your calendar.

In the next chapter I will introduce another subset of Chrome apps for creating documents of various kinds, after first describing the Google Drive cloud-based file storage system.

Google Drive, Docs, Sheets and Slides

In the brave new world of cloud computing, all your documents and other files are stored "in the cloud" on a server computer at the other end of your internet connection rather than being stored locally on your PC hard drive. The idea is that you can access your files anytime from anywhere using any device that has an internet connection and which runs the Chrome web browser.

Google Drive

In the Google cloud computing world, the home to your files on the internet is Google Drive.

Navigating Google Drive

You can access your Google Drive by selecting the triangular Google Drive app from the chromebook launcher or by clicking the same triangular icon on the app shelf at the bottom of the screen.

If you don't have a Google Drive icon on the shelf, you can add it by right-clicking or long-pressing the app in the app tray and selecting the "pin to shelf" option.

Alternatively, you can always access your Google Drive by typing drive.google.com into the Chrome browser's omnibox.

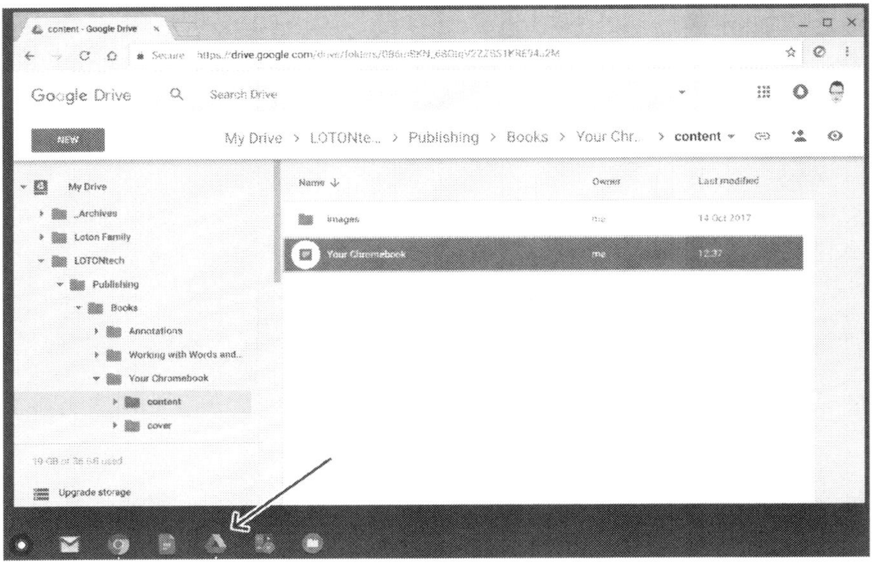

You can navigate your Google Drive folders in the left-hand column and see the contents of the currently-selected folder to the right—which is very much the same as using a local file explorer such as Windows File Explorer or even the chromebook Files app, except that this file explorer is on the web. In the previous picture I have selected a folder named 'content' which contains the content (manuscript and images) for the book you are reading now.

When using the web-based Google Drive you can perform the kinds of file manipulation tasks that you are used to; for example, dragging files from one folder to another or renaming files (by right-clicking and choosing the "rename" option from the pop-up context menu). You can click the NEW button (see previous picture) to create new folders, Docs, Sheets or Slides, or to upload a file or folder from your local computer to the web-based Drive.

In the left column of your Google Drive, beneath "My Drive", you will see a "Shared with me" link that can be clicked to see the list of files that have been shared with you from other people's Google Drives.

Accessing Google Drive from Other Devices

At this point it's worth reminding you that you can access your web-based Google Drive from any computer or other device that runs a web browser; ideally Google Chrome. But on specific devices such as your Windows PC, or your Android phone or tablet, there are other ways of interacting with Google Drive via the Google Drive "Backup and Sync" program (Windows) or Drive app (Android).

You can access your Google Drive on the web via your chromebook either by typing drive.google.com into a browser tab or by selecting the Google Drive app icon as already discussed. You can also access your Google Drive on your chromebook via the Files app, which provides a convenient way for you to copy files such as pictures and other non-Google files to your online Google Drive from another source such as a USB stick or from your Downloads folder.

Note that when you access your Google Drive via the Files app, you may not automatically be able to open a file from your Google Drive when you are offline (not connected to the internet) until you have marked the file as available offline. You need to be online in order to mark files as available offline – so that they can be automatically copied to your chromebook – but of course this should not be necessary for files that originated on your chromebook in the first place.

Photos-Drive Integration

One of the things I had to do during the creation of this book is to take photos using my Android mobile phone and then edit them from my chromebook using the online Pixlr Editor. The process for getting those photos off the phone and into the online picture editor was as follows:

1. Any photos taken on my phone are automatically uploaded to my Google Photos library, which can be accessed as a pseudo-folder from Google Drive **(1)**.
2. For any selected photo, I can formally "Add to My Drive" **(2)**.
3. Any such photo added to my Google Drive can then be opened directly with the Pixlr Editor **(3)**.

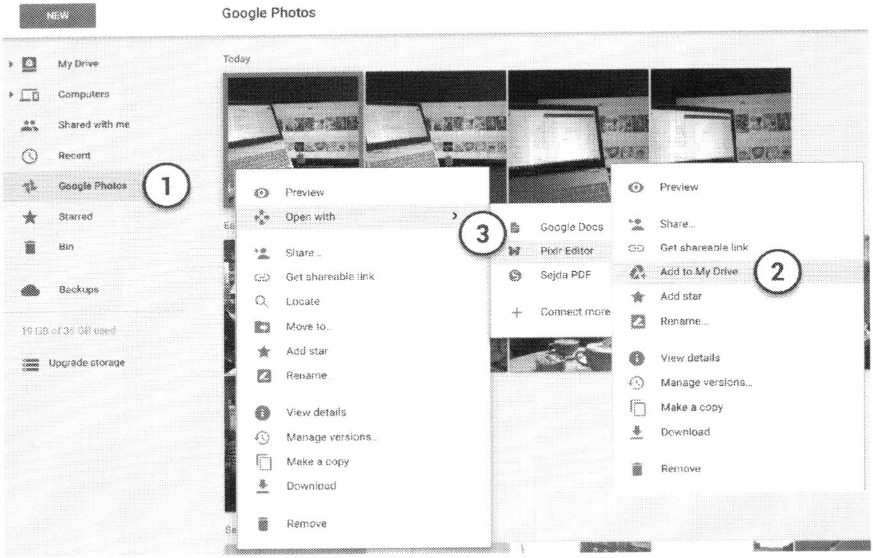

Note that this sleight of hand is achieved via the Google Drive web app, not from the Google Photos web app.

Google Docs, Sheets and Slides

I've told you about Google Drive, and how it is possible to use its web interface to create new Google-format documents, spreadsheets, presentations and other files in your drive. This ability to create and edit various office documents is what is often collectively called "Google Docs". Google Docs is the office suite that you will be using by default on your web-only chromebook, but it's not the only option... as you will see.

When you click the Google Drive NEW button, you can create new Google Docs, Sheets and Slides as well as new folders. Let's look at each of the file types – docs, sheets and slides – in turn.

Google Docs

The first and most useful office file type that you can create in your Google Drive is the Google Doc (or Google Document).

As a freelance writer for several publications, I have used Google Docs to write feature articles and share them with journal editors without going anywhere near Microsoft Word. As a tool for writing linear articles with alternating text and pictures, it is perfectly acceptable, and I even wrote entire first edition and most of the third edition of my original chromebook book as a Google Document.

As an e-book creation tool, Google Docs is perfectly acceptable. As a tool for producing professionally formatted book manuscripts and converting these to print-ready Portable Document Format (PDF) files to be published in paperback format, it is fast catching up with Microsoft Word providing you're willing to make just a few manuscript creation compromises. To prove my point, I have not resorted to Word at all during the creation of the book you are reading now.

If you must still use Microsoft Word, you will find it perfectly possible to store Word documents in your Google Drive, and you can even edit those documents in the Chrome browser using Microsoft Word Online. If all else fails, the real Microsoft Word and other Windows programs can be accessed remotely from a legacy PC (which could even be on the other side of the world) via the Chrome Remote Desktop feature.

The Google Docs Screen

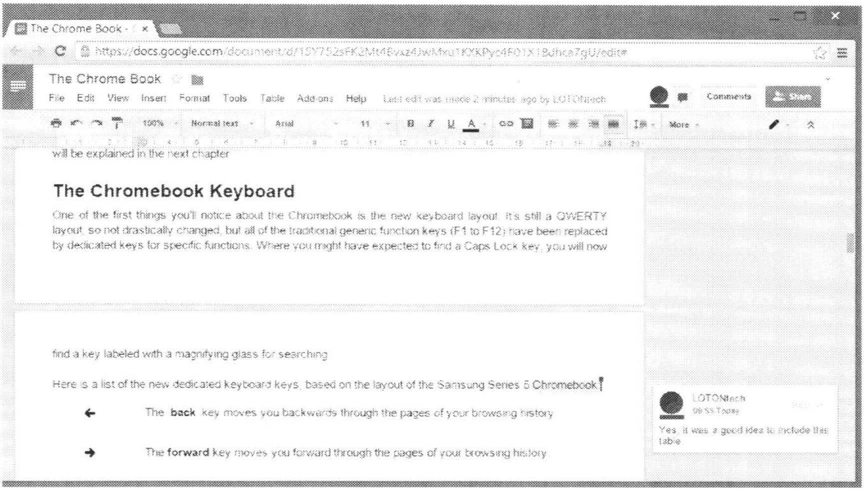

Let me now give you an idea of what you can achieve with a Google Docs document. As just stated, I've re-authored this book entirely within Google Docs. As proof, the previous figure shows a section of the book manuscript (as a Google Document) comprising a styled heading followed by alternating text and graphics. You can also see in this figure how one of my colleagues has commented on the document using the collaboration features of Google Docs that will be discussed shortly.

This document editing interface, with a set of menus and buttons across the top of the document you are editing, will be very familiar to users of Microsoft Word and other word processors. As such, I won't provide a "for dummies" tutorial or blow-by-blow account of every option here, but you will find some useful document creation and editing information in my later case study chapter. I do, however, have a few less-obvious things to say.

Google Docs Preferences

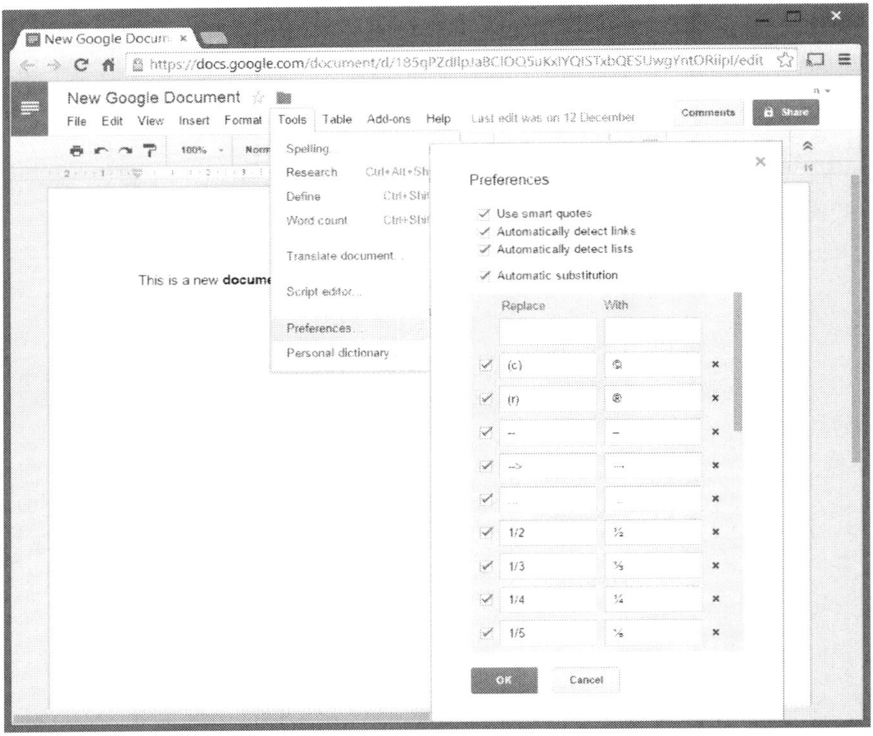

One thing you might notice in this book is that I am quite keen on using N-dashes or M-dashes (basically long hyphens) to demark a sub-phrase – like this one – within a longer sentence. It's easy in Microsoft Word because I just have to type a word, then a space and two regular hyphens, then a space and the next word, in order to see those two regular hyphens converted automatically into a longer dash. It's just as easy in Google Docs to enable or disable this kind of automatic substitution – which might also include converting the text "(c)" to the copyright symbol "©" – via the Google Docs Preferences that can be accessed via the Tools menu; see previous picture.

Exporting Google Docs

Even though *you* may be moving to the cloud, not everyone else will have done so just yet, so some people – like the magazine editors with whom I sometimes work – will still be expecting you to provide them with documents in Microsoft Word format. You can convert any Google Docs document to Microsoft Word (.docx) format and other popular formats such as Portable Document Format (.pdf) by choosing "Download as" from the File menu.

Tracking Revisions

Have you ever made changes to a document, and saved it, but then wished you could go back to the original version... or to a much earlier version? One really neat feature of Google Docs is the ability to do just that by choosing the "Version history" option from the File menu. In the following picture you can see the latest version of this book manuscript, with the most recent changed text highlighted. From the revision history to the right it is possible (for example) to restore the last-but-one version that didn't include this change.

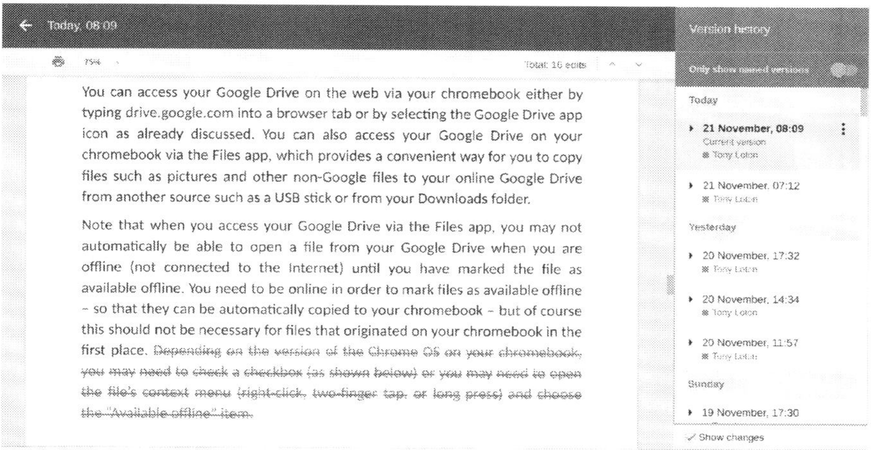

This kind of page history will be very familiar to anyone who has used a commercial Wiki-like technical authoring system such as Confluence. Unlike Confluence, Google Docs allows you to rename particular page versions so that you can (for example) keep track of major milestones such as the versions of a manuscript that were published as 'editions' of a book:

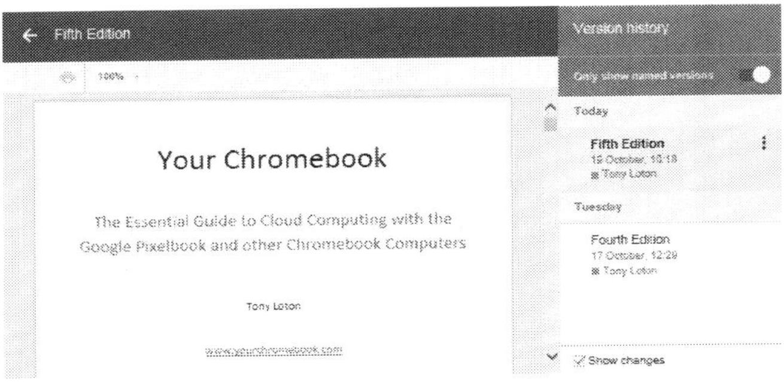

Google Sheets

Sheets is Google's online equivalent of the Microsoft Excel spreadsheet program. If you're familiar will spreadsheets, you will find it quite intuitive, and if not then I defer to other good books for a comprehensive tutorial.

I will, however, provide an example of how powerful the Google Sheets web app can be...

Google Sheets Spreadsheet Example

While I found the original incarnations of the Google Docs word processor a little limiting (but now much less so), the Google Sheets offering has always lived up to what I would expect from a spreadsheet program. I have been able to devise spreadsheets that use formulas, functions and cell references, and which retain most if not all of these when converting to and from Microsoft Excel (.xlsx) format.

The spreadsheet shown below is one that I created as an example for financial traders who hope to re-enter a stock position at a lower price than the price at which they last sold. *Note that the problem that this spreadsheet solves is not as important as the techniques it utilizes.*

3	Symbol	Price	Last Stop-Out	Want to...	Change Since Stop	%Change Since Stop	Open Signal	%Change Today	Info & Chart
25	HAS.L	111.048	107.74	Long	3.31	3.07%		-1.64%	http://uk.financ
26	HDY.L	208.4	216	Long	-7.60	-3.52%	3.52%	-0.29%	http://uk.financ
27	HSD.L	157	160	Long	-3.00	-1.88%		-1.88%	http://uk.financ
28	INCH.L	377.8	299	Long	78.80	26.35%		-3.60%	http://uk.financ
29	IFL.L	20	19	Long	1.00	5.26%		1.27%	http://uk.financ
30	IPR.L	317.3	335	Long	-17.70	-5.28%	5.28%	-2.28%	http://uk.financ
31	IPO.L	49.5	29	Long	20.50	70.69%		3.13%	http://uk.financ
32	IPF.L	353.2	238	Long	115.20	48.40%		-3.42%	http://uk.financ
33	ITV.L	69.7	49	Long	20.70	42.24%		-1.48%	http://uk.financ
34	JJB.L	25	35	Long	-10.00	-28.57%	28.57%	-1.96%	http://uk.financ
35	JKX.L	288.7	285	Long	3.70	1.30%		-1.37%	http://uk.financ

In this spreadsheet the user is able to enter a Stock Symbol in the first column, with this cell entry being used to fetch live data from the World Wide Web using the following formula:

```
=ImportData("http://download.finance.yahoo.com/d/quotes.csv?f=sl1d1
t1c1ohgv&e=.csv&s="&$A26)
```

This is pretty powerful stuff, which replicates the Microsoft Excel capability for retrieving web data using a web query.

The live price retrieved into the second column is compared with the user-entered "Last Stop-Out" (i.e. last selling price) in the third column so as to calculate and color-code the % Change in the sixth column. This demonstrates the ability to apply *conditional formatting* to cell contents.

In the final "Info & Chart" column the user-entered Stock Symbol has been formulated into a web address URL that links to the stock's chart on the Yahoo! Finance web site (sorry Google) thus demonstrating the spreadsheet string manipulation functions.

It's just one example, which I offer here to show that it really is possible to do with the Google Docs spreadsheet pretty much all of the things you would have done with Microsoft Excel. This includes the ability to produce charts from your data as illustrated below; and via Google Drive you are able to publish your chart to a unique web address URL by clicking the "Publish chart" button that you can see in the picture.

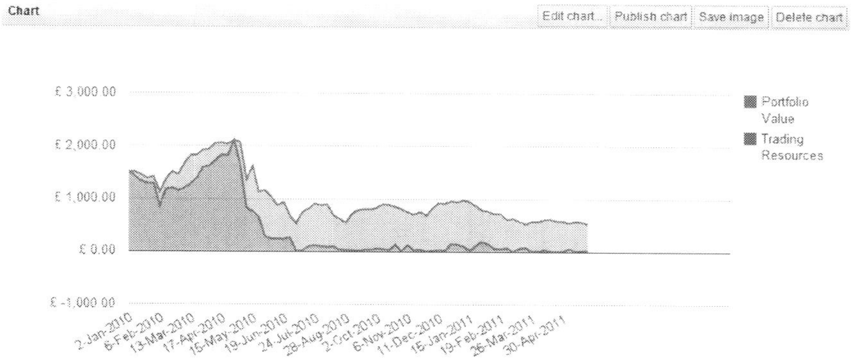

Docs and Sheets Common Functionality

One thing to bear in mind is that there is a lot of functionality that is common to Google Docs and Google Sheets; for example the ability to track revisions and the ability to collaborate by sharing your spreadsheets with other users by clicking the Share button at the top-right of the screen and entering one or more email addresses.

Google Slides

If you're familiar with creating electronic presentations using a program such as Microsoft PowerPoint, you'll be at home creating presentations using Google Slides. It's a worthy alternative to PowerPoint, and it's getting better all the time, but don't (yet) expect to be able to do all of the things that PowerPoint allows you to do. Also be aware that if you upload existing PowerPoint presentations to your Google Drive, some of the layout may well be lost in the translation.

With the bad news out of the way, let me tell you the good news:

The Benefits of Cloud-Based Presentations

The idea of creating presentations "in the cloud" is a perfectly sound idea. Most presentations are created to be taken somewhere for showing, usually to some corporate venue. Some presenters have found themselves in the unfortunate position of having somehow lost, while traveling, the USB drive, DVD, or even laptop that contained the presentation. With your presentation in the cloud, you have no such worry. You can access it from your clients' computers in their offices or boardrooms with no possibility of losing anything in transit. As long as your client provides you with access to a web browser, that is.

When did you last attend a 'live' presentation anyway? Haven't you noticed that many of the seminars that you would previously have attended in person have now been replaced with online 'webinars'? It makes sense if you want to reach an even wider international audience, and in this context the ability to embed a Google Slides presentation in a web page is one of the most useful features. Just choose "Publish to the web... / embed" from the File menu as shown here:

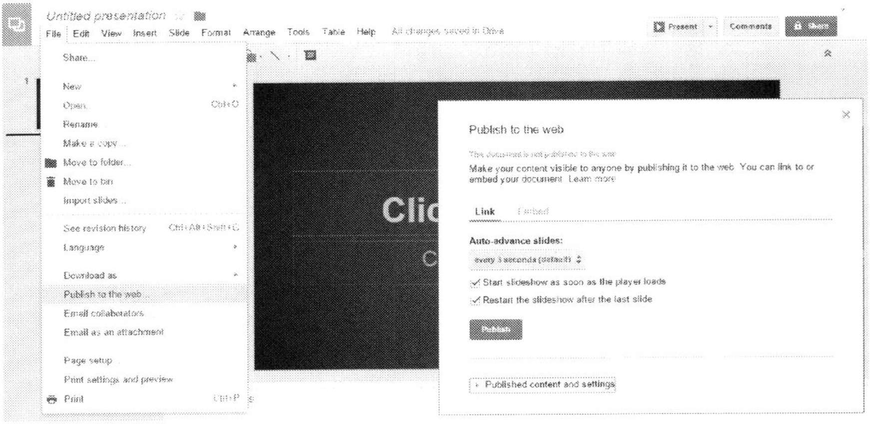

Once you have published the presentation to a unique web address URL for all to see (so beware) you can copy the embedding code that begins "<iframe src=" into your Blogger blog or other website so as to embed the presentation in the same way that you might embed a YouTube video.

If you ever want to make the presentation unavailable, you can always click the "Stop publishing" button that is accessible via the "File / Publish to the web..." menu option.

Presenting on the "Big Screen"

Although Slides makes it easy to create web-based presentations, many of us still create presentations with a view to "presenting" them live while standing in front of a big screen. You will find instructions on connecting a chromebook to a big screen TV (or potentially a projector with a HDMI input) in the Google Play chapter of this book... because that's where I tell you how to attach to a big screen for the purpose of playing movies.

Not Just Docs, Sheets and Slides

The Google Drive document types that can be created via the NEW button are not limited to Docs, Sheets and Slides. You can create other kinds of files including Forms and Drawings.

Google Forms

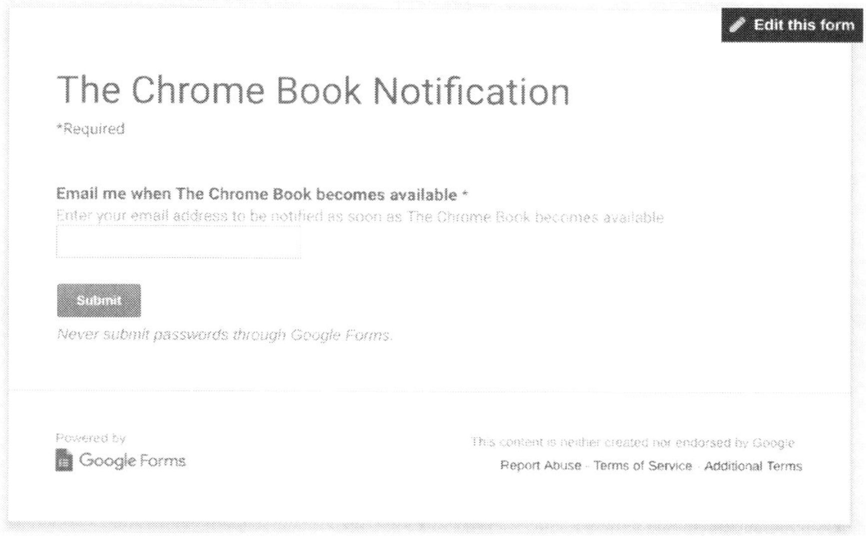

Google Forms can be surprisingly useful for embedding into your website or blog to collect information from your visitors. The previous picture shows a very simple form that I created some time ago, so that in the run up to my book's initial release, my blog visitors could sign up to be notified as soon as the book became available.

It's a simple form with only one textbox for user input, but I can tell you that it is also possible to include pick lists and choice buttons in the forms you create.

My daughter used Google Forms to conduct more comprehensive surveys while studying for her Creative Media diploma, which was facilitated by the fact that you can send forms to email addresses. Another useful application I have found for Google Forms is the provision of a web site "contact me" form as an alternative to publicly displaying an email address.

Each form that you create has a complementary spreadsheet, which is populated with a new entry each time a visitor submits your form. So, for my book notification example the responses spreadsheet might look like this:

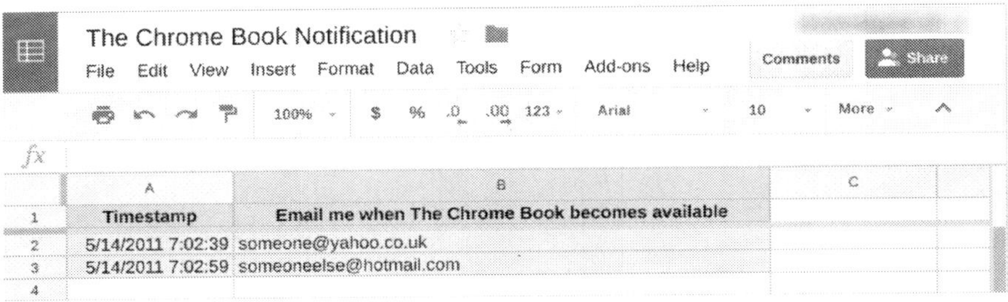

This basic form functionality will be most suited to those of you who want to add a degree of interactivity to your website or blog without learning the necessary HTML code or other web programming techniques. And to get you started, there are handy templates for common forms like Contact Information, RSVP and Party Invite.

Google Drawing

A Google Drawing provides a canvas for you to combine images, text and other elements into composite creations.

In at least one of the earlier editions of this book, I used a Google Drawing to create the cover art for this book, just to show that I could. I don't do that now, but I do sometimes find myself deferring to the Drawing capability when I can't easily do what I want to do within Google Docs itself.

For example, I recently needed to compose some Word Art text with a color gradient for the cover of a client's book. Neither Google Docs nor (surprisingly) the Pixlr Editor were up to the job, but a Google Drawing allowed me to do exactly what I wanted to do:

One good thing about the Google Drawing tool is that all of the photographs, text boxes and other graphical elements you place are at all times individually selectable (like when using Microsoft PowerPoint) rather than being "baked into" the final image as they would be when using a rasterized drawing tool like Microsoft Paint. So you can move, resize, and otherwise arrange them to your heart's content when using a Google Drawing.

You can start a new drawing by choosing Drawing from the NEW pull-down menu in your Google Drive.

Sharing Docs, Sheets and Slides

One of the big benefits of an online office suite compared with traditional standalone office software is the ability to collaborate on documents, spreadsheets and other files. The first step toward collaborating is to share your document, spreadsheet, presentation, or drawing by clicking the Share button at the top-right of the screen **(1 below)**. You can also share any item within a folder, or an entire folder, by right-clicking the item in the Google Drive browser (not shown) and choosing the Share option. In all cases, you should see the "Share settings" dialog **(2)**:

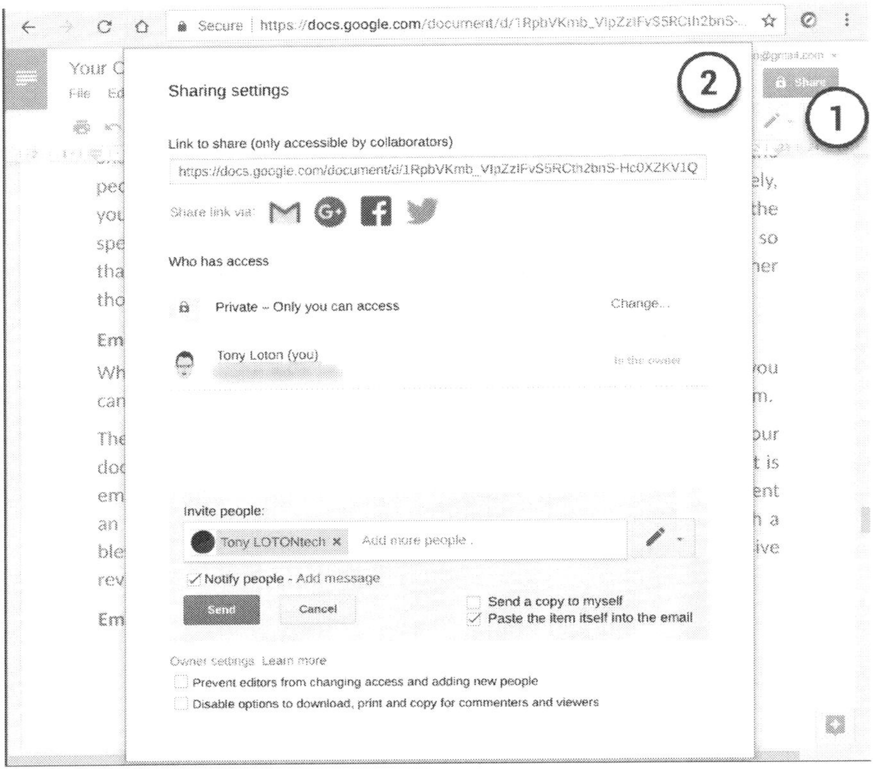

Sharing settings allow you to make an item private so that only you and the people you specify can access it (if they are signed in to Google). Alternatively, you can make an item available to "Anyone with the link" (if you tell them the specific web address URL of the item) or you can make it "Public to the Web" so that it shows up in web searches. In all three cases you can decide whether those who have access can edit the item or merely view it.

Email Editors / Viewers

Where you have entered a specific list of collaborators for a private item, you can notify people via email with a message that also contains a link to the item.

The people you have deemed to be editors can post comments to your document as well as making changes to its content. Every posted comment is emailed to the document owner, and whenever the owner resolves a comment an email is sent to the editor who posted the comment. This can be both a blessing and a curse, as it can soon clog up your Inbox during an extensive reviewing and editing cycle.

Email as attachment...

In some cases you won't want to send out a hyperlink to the live item, but instead you will want to email a copy of the item as an attachment in a specific format like Microsoft Word (.docx) format. I would do this when submitting a written article to a magazine editor.

It's exactly like emailing a document or other file as an attachment as you would usually do, but now you're attaching it straight from the cloud and emailing it using your Gmail email address. This is important because you are not using valuable bandwidth by downloading the file over the internet to your own computer or chromebook simply to send it out again over the internet.

Publish to the Web...

You can also choose to publish any Google Docs document to the web by choosing the "Publish to the web..." option from the document File menu.

A copy of the file will be published with a unique web address URL, and this copy can be refreshed (optionally) when changes are made to the original. Thus you might provide the general public with temporary access to a copy of your document without giving away the location of the original; and you can unpublish the copy whenever you like.

Offline Docs, Sheets and Slides

One of the issues with the original web-based Google Docs office suite was the fact that you had to be online in order to edit your documents. Having no internet connection on your chromebook meant that you had no access to your documents; and a lost internet connection while editing a document meant that your changes would be lost.

Things have improved to the extent that, when you are disconnected, Google Drive will now report "You are offline. Some functionality may be unavailable".

To allow for a degree of offline editing, you need to make sure that within the Google Drive Settings **(1)** the Offline option **(2)** is enabled to cache local copies of files on your chromebook or other computer as shown next.

Note that because this feature will make copies of your Google Drive files on the computer's local hard disk, it is not recommended when using a shared or public Windows PC.

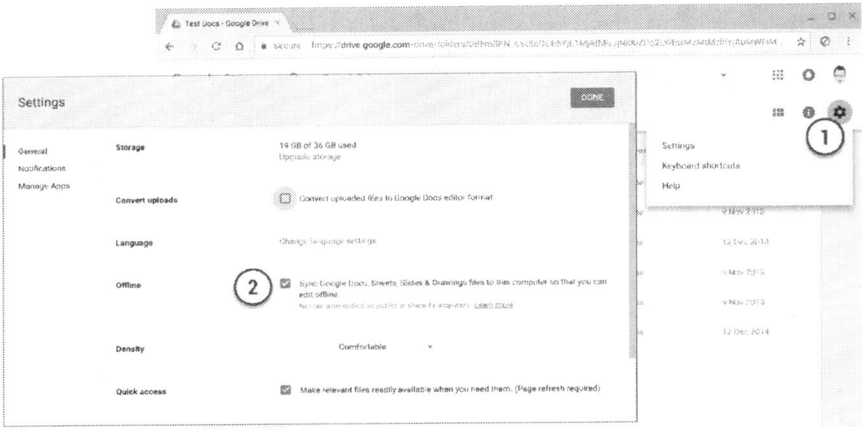

Only Applies to Google Docs

You'll know when you're editing a document offline because you'll see the "You are offline" indication at the top of the screen. Here is an example of a Google Document being edited while Docs is reporting that "You are offline".

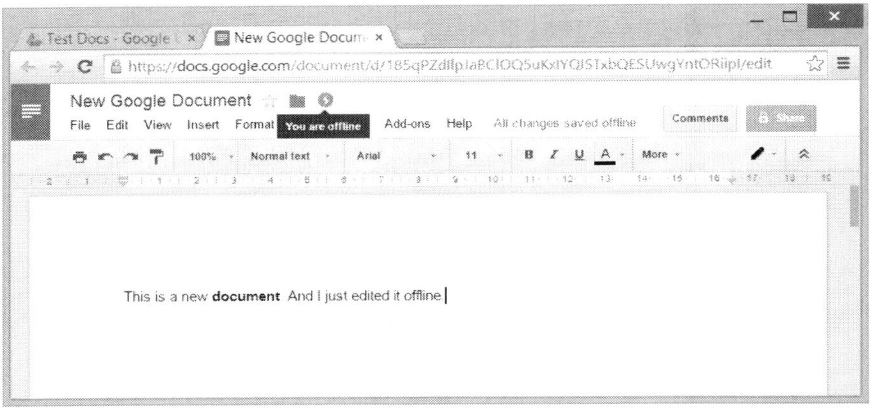

Upon reconnecting to the internet, the document is re-synced and reports "All changes saved in Drive". Once you're up-and-running it should be pretty seamless because the Chrome web browser will detect whether or not you have an internet connection, and will put you into online or offline mode as appropriate.

This Offline Docs feature only applies to your Google-format documents, but if you've installed the Google Drive Backup & Sync software to your PC, you can always edit your regular Microsoft Word documents (or Excel spreadsheets, or anything else) in the usual way when offline. They will be re-synced with Google Drive when you are next connected.

Google Drive Docs Advantages and Disadvantages

Now you have some idea of how Google Drive works and what you can do with it. But why would you want to use it? What does Google Docs (including Sheets and Slides) give you that the traditional PC office suite doesn't... or at least didn't? Here are some suggestions:

- Your open documents are saved automatically at regular intervals, so you don't have to become obsessive-compulsive about pressing the CTRL-S keyboard combination every few minutes in case your PC crashes. Yes, I have suffered in the past from CTRL-S obsessive-compulsive disorder... and for very good reason.
- Your stored documents have a complete revision history. If you make a mistake, you can roll-back to a previous version by choosing "See revision history" from the File menu.
- Since your documents are stored online in the cloud (i.e. on a Google server computer) you can access them from any computer anywhere via a web browser.
- You can easily share your documents with viewers and collaborators without resorting to sending them as email attachments.
- It's free! At least for individuals.

The Microsoft OneDrive Alternative to Google Drive and Docs

Since Chrome is merely a web browser running on your chromebook, PC or other device, you are not restricted to using Google Docs as your online office suite.

For some time I was a fan of the Adobe Buzzword online word processor that never really caught on (and maybe no longer exists); and for something rather more mainstream you might try the Microsoft Office online apps - including online versions of Word and Excel - that are accessible via the Microsoft OneDrive (which is more-or-less the Microsoft equivalent of the Google Drive) at onedrive.live.com.

If you already have a Microsoft Office 365 subscription, which for some reason I still do, then it may be something of a "no-brainer" to use the online versions of the Microsoft Office programs such as Word, Excel and PowerPoint. And doing so won't invalidate everything you've read in this book because you can still use the Chrome web browser on your chromebook or (even more logically) on your PC. So you'll still be practicing cloud computing with Chrome, but Microsoft's rather than Google's version of cloud computing.

Here is a picture of the manuscript for one of the editions of this book being edited using the Microsoft Word Online web app running in the Chrome browser:

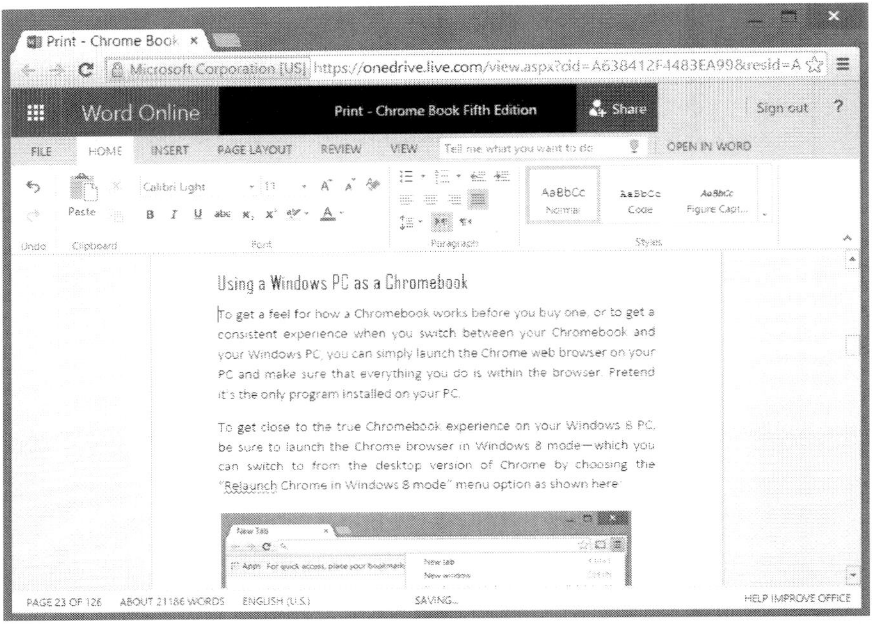

The web app is more limited than the PC-installed version of Microsoft Word, and is in no way a complete replacement, but it is a worthy alternative to the Google Docs word processor for the creation of ebooks and other simple documents. Similar things might be said of the Microsoft Excel and Microsoft PowerPoint web apps when use for their respective purposes.

Depending on your needs, you might also find some handy third party office apps in the Chrome Web Store.

Using Google Drive to Store and Edit Microsoft Office Files

Wait a minute! The plot thickens, and you do not necessarily need to resort to Microsoft's OneDrive in order to work with Word documents and other Microsoft Office files. You can use your Google Drive to store or backup any or all of your files on the web, even if they're not Google-format documents.

To upload a file to your Google Drive, all you need to do is click the "File upload" icon and then select the required file from the PC or chromebook file system (e.g. your chromebook Downloads folder or an attached USB stick). Be sure to have selected the required Google Drive destination folder first.

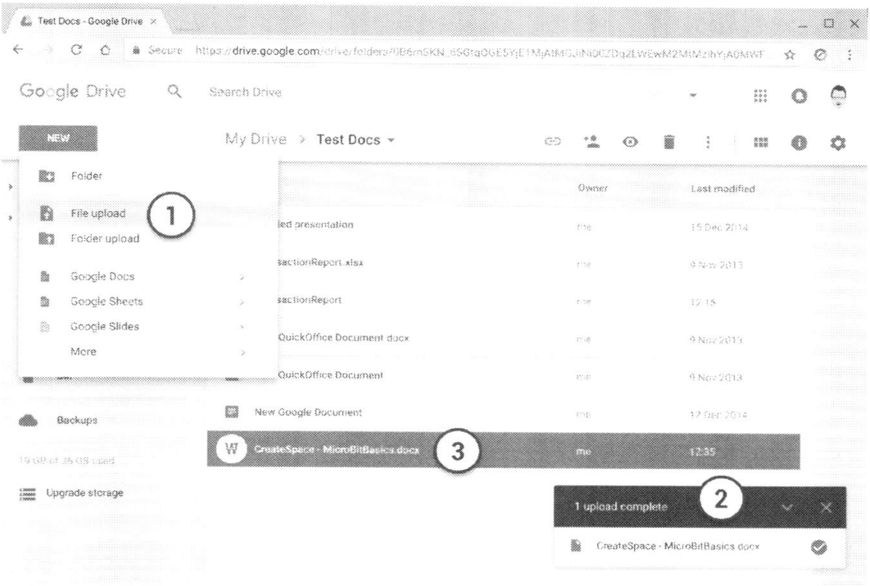

Any Word documents uploaded to Google Drive can be edited directly in Google Docs, but I find this facility to be ostensibly less impressive than I might like. Comparing the exact same Word document being edited using Google Docs (left below) and Word Online (right below) I see some notable differences in terms of fonts, page breaks and other aspects:

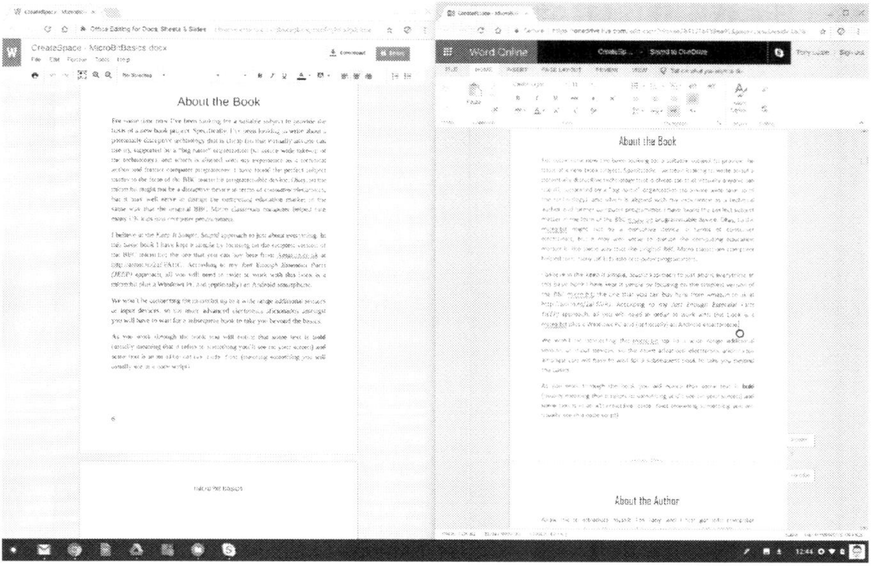

The differences between the Google Docs and Word Online renderings of the same Word document made me nervous in case they became permanent in the edited and saved document, but here's the good news...

From my cursory experiments, I deduced that - after editing a Word document in Google Docs, saving it (which is automatic), and then re-syncing the file back to my PC hard disk - the integrity of the original Word document is preserved when reopened in the bona fide Microsoft Word on the PC.

In this respect, the editing of Word documents in Google Docs appears to work the same way as the Word Online web app. In both cases, the web app provides a limited set of functionality and imperfect rendering of documents, but allows you to edit a subset of the document content while leaving the unsupported aspects of the document intact.

Chapter Summary

In this chapter I have introduced the Google Drive cloud-based online storage; detailing how you navigate it and how you can use it to create and arrange the various Google-format "office" files: Docs (documents), Sheets (spreadsheets), Slides (presentations), Forms (as the name suggests), and Drawings.

I have also explained how you can use Google Drive to store, backup, and even edit your non-Google files such as Microsoft Office documents.

Music, Movies, Books and Google Play

Apart from a few vintage vinyl fans and compact disc collectors, gone are the days of people buying their music on physical media. Music has gone digital, and so have movies and (to some extent) books. So this chapter is about purchasing and managing your digital media via the Google Play Store.

Unlike the Amazon Kindle, possibly the Apple iPad, and even the ill-fated Microsoft Surface "RT version" (the what?) which we may regard as mainly media-playing devices, Google chromebooks are not targeted specifically at consumers of ebooks, movies, music and other media. Nonetheless, it is perfectly possible to use a chromebook as a media machine, or to use the Google Play Store as the source of media content on any device that runs the Chrome web browser.

In the chromebook's app launcher you should already find icons for Google's Play Music, Play Movies, Play Books, and Play Games services; plus an icon for the Play Store app itself:

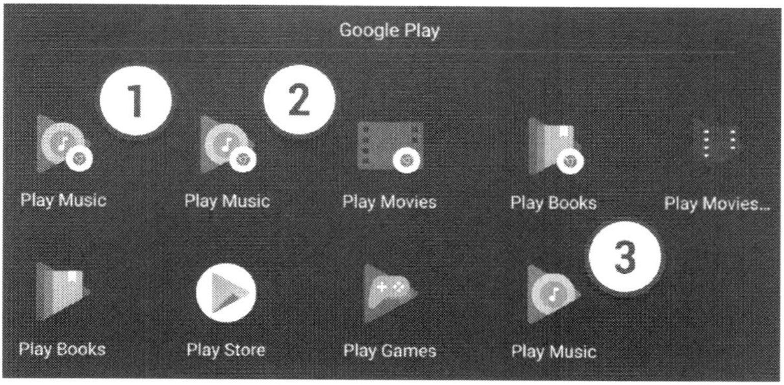

You might wonder why there is more than one icon for Play Music (not to mention Play Movies and Play Books) so I'll do my best to explain.

Google Play Music

In the previous picture, the three Play Music app icons, in order, are:

(1) The mini music player, for which you need to be signed in to Google Play Music on the web.

(2) The online Play Music web app, for which you need to be connected to the internet. *Think of this as similar to the online Google Drive web app, but for your music.*

(3) The chromebook's locally installed Play Music Android app which allows you to play downloaded music when offline. *Think of this as similar to the chromebook Files app, but for music.*

The Android app allows you to access music from your online library plus any tunes you have stored on the device itself. In the following picture I can tell you that the Muse song "The Resistance" is one that I downloaded to my device from my Amazon Music account, and the Kate Bush album is one which I have downloaded in the same way as I am about to download Queen's "A Day At The Races" using the context menu's Download option. In the second picture below, I have thrown the switch to show "Downloaded only" in the Android app:

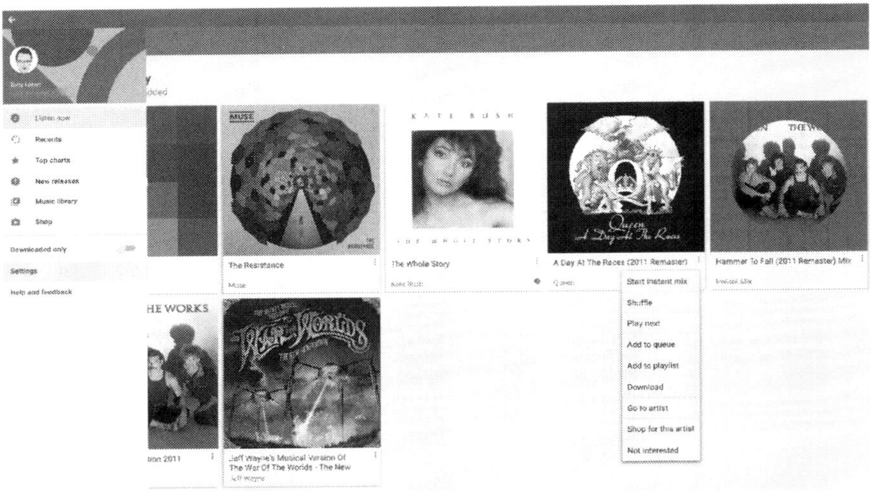

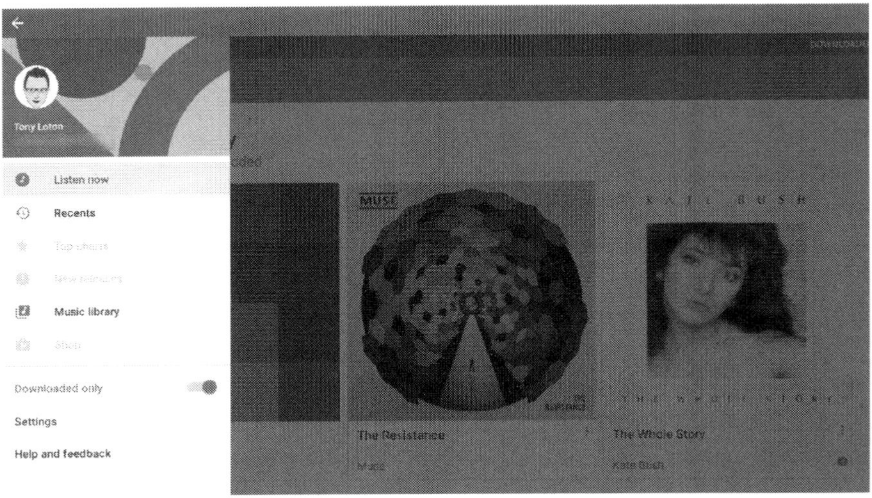

Shopping for Music

The Google Play Music storefront at play.google.com/store/music is where you can shop for new music. You can purchase individual tracks or albums, or sign up for one of the monthly music plans. You can also preview potential purchases, and I have to admit to getting a lot of mileage out of occasionally playing a whole album's worth of preview snippets.

As already stated, albums that you have purchased can be streamed direct from the internet via Play Music in Chrome browser, or they can be downloaded for playing when offline. As with other Google Play content, you can play your purchased tracks on other compatible devices such as on your Android phone or tablet.

Uploading Music

You can upload music from your device to your Google Play library online, which is what I did with the Muse song I had previously downloaded from my Amazon Music account:

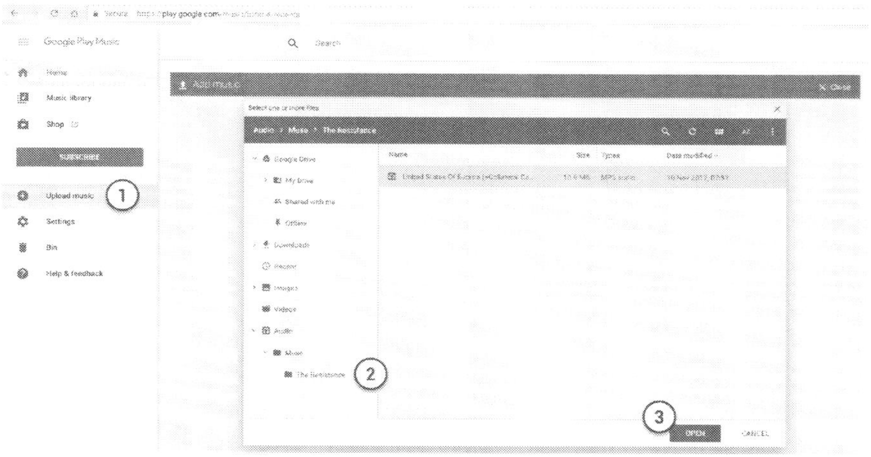

Google Play Movies and TV

Play Movies is pretty much the same as Play Music in terms of there being a Chrome web app / web site (top picture below) and an equivalent Android app (bottom picture below), both of which allow you to stream or download movies from your library:

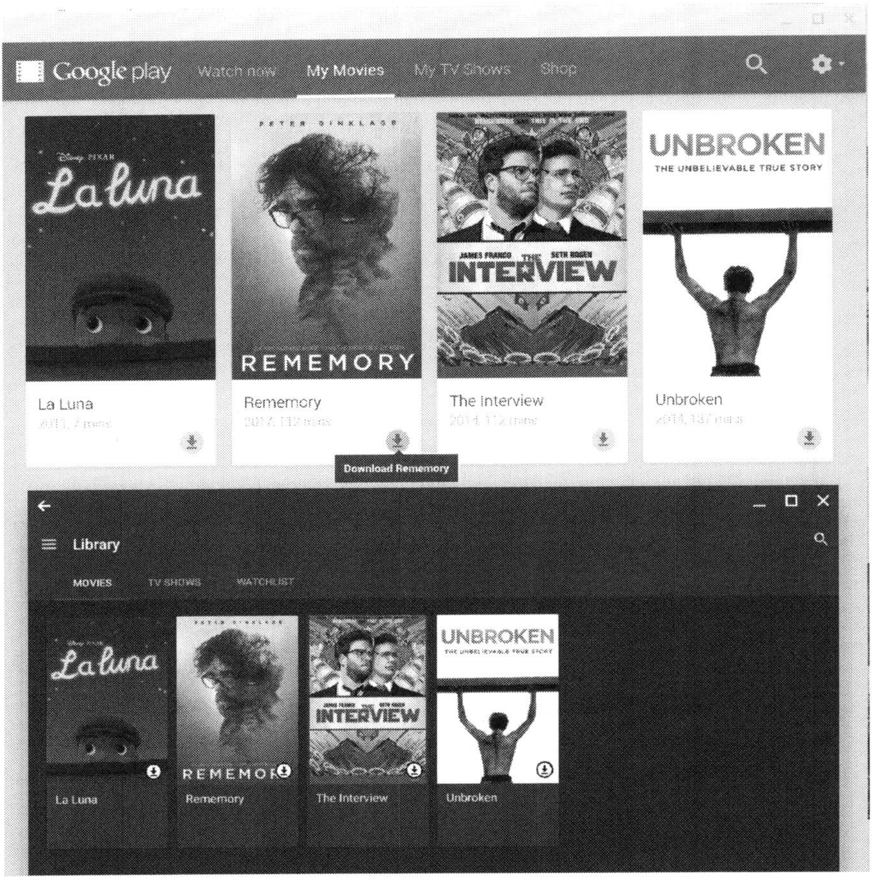

The Play Movies and TV store at play.google.com/store/movies allows you to rent movies for 48 hours as well as purchase them to keep in the cloud forever.

Any movies and TV that you purchase from Google Play on your chromebook or PC can also be played from your Android mobile phone or tablet, and vice versa. But in order to download a movie to a second device (e.g. your Android phone) you might need to remove it from your other device (e.g. your chromebook) first.

Attaching a Chromebook to a Big Screen TV

Although you can watch video content on your chromebook screen, you will most likely want to watch your movies on a "big screen" TV. In the following picture you can see how I have my Google Pixelbook connected to a TV via a USB-C-to-HDMI adapter, and how I have extended the desktop so that I can use

Google Play on the TV screen (i.e. to watch a movie) while at the same time editing this book's manuscript in Google Docs on the chromebook itself:

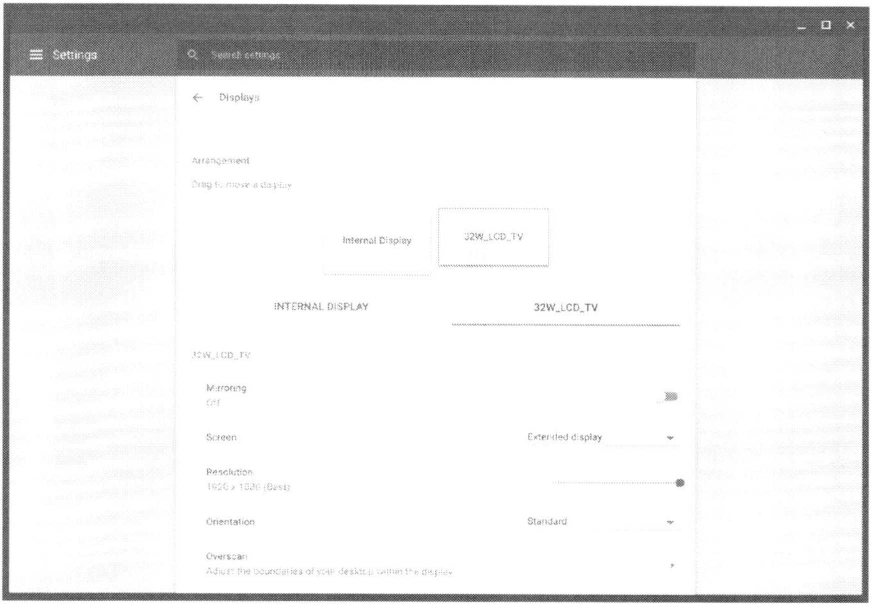

You can set the chromebook screen to extend to the right (as just described) or simply to mirror what is shown on the chromebook screen, and you can easily switch between the two modes by pressing **ctrl +**  on the chromebook keyboard. You can also manage the display settings from within your chromebook's Settings as shown above.

An alternative for displaying media content on a "big screen" TV is to use Google's Chromecast device as discussed next.

Chromecast

Chromecast is Google's media streaming device that plugs into any TV via the HDMI port (as shown below) and turns it into a "smart" TV.

Chromecast devices now look a little different from when I first took this picture of one, but the principle is still the same.

You can use a Chromecast to cast movies, songs, other media and browser tabs from your chromebook, or the Chrome browser on your PC, or from your Android device, onto the "big screen". While this Google Play chapter is the most logical place to discuss Chromecast, do keep in mind that the functionality is not limited to casting Google Play Movies onto a TV screen.

Before casting to Chromecast device you'll need to set it up by visiting chromecast.com/setup in the Chrome browser. Although you can download the Chromecast Android app, it's easier to set things up from your chromebook simply by clicking the link labelled "set up your chromecast using this computer".

When your Chromecast device declares itself ready to cast, you can henceforth choose the Cast option from the Chrome pull-down menu **(1)** then choose whether to cast a browser tab or the whole desktop **(2)**.

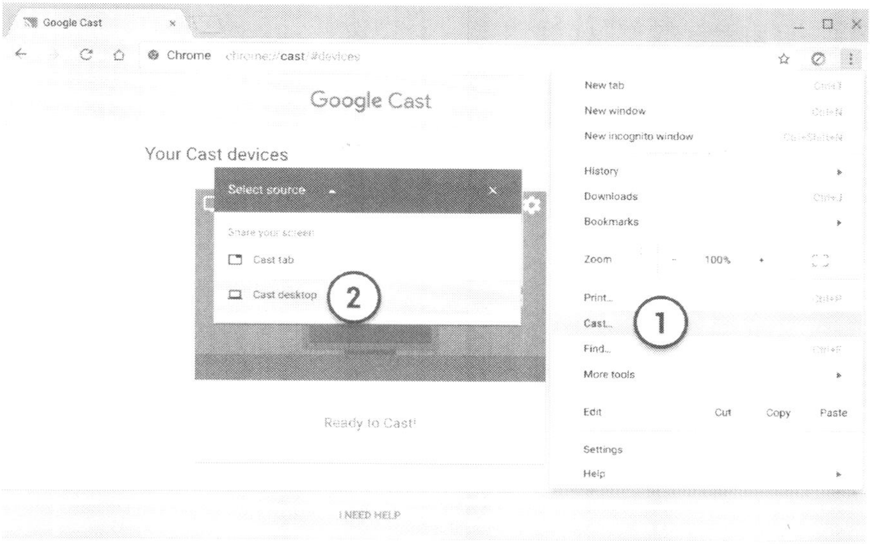

Casting the entire desktop or a browser tab in this way can be useful, but it's not the most efficient way to cast movie content to your TV screen.

Wherever you see the Chromecast symbol on video content, you can click to cast the video to your TV. This might be YouTube videos, Google Play Movies, or movie trailers such as the one shown here:

When you cast video in this way, only the moving images are transmitted to the TV screen—not the entire contents of the browser tab. In fact, in most if not all cases the browser will display a static placeholder image (as shown above) but with a pause icon and other controls displayed so that you can control the playback from your chromebook or other device running the Chrome browser.

You can also cast music that you have purchased from the Google Play Store, as shown here:

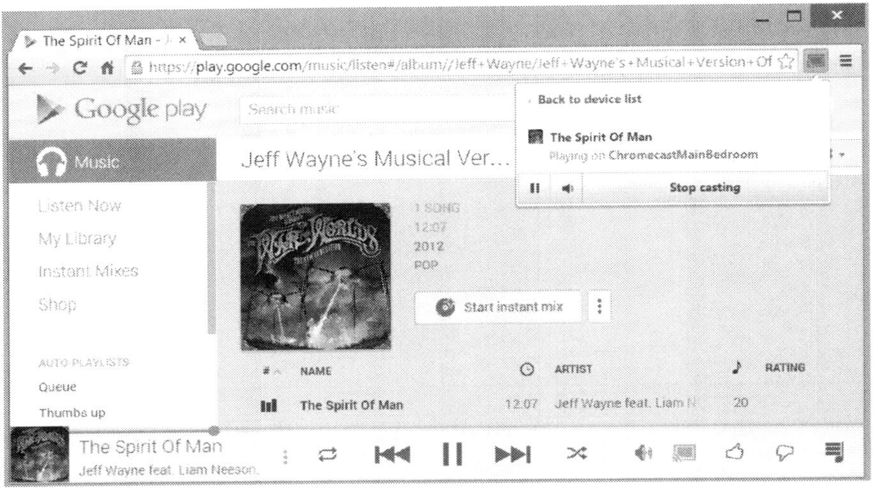

Now seems to be a good time to say that, when it comes to playing video content on your chromebook or through the Chrome browser on your PC, Google Play is not the only source.

The next most obvious source of videos is Google's YouTube service that features mainly user-generated, or at least user-uploaded, content rather than professionally produced movies and TV shows. You can find the YouTube app in the Chrome Web Store (if it's not already installed) or you can simply visit www.youtube.com in the Chrome browser. You could even use YouTube to upload your own video creations, but it's beyond the scope of this book.

You will find a plethora of big-name and not-so-big-name movie and TV apps in the Chrome Web Store, and you can use many other web-based video services, so you're not limited to Google Play. There are a few caveats, because some video services (e.g. iTunes) may not be compatible with the chromebook and some others may depend on technology such as Microsoft's Silverlight plugin to play videos.

Google Play Books

As Google's equivalent of Amazon's Kindle book service, Play Books acts as your book collection in the cloud.

You know the routine now. For Google Play Books there is a web app icon that leads to books.google.com/ebooks/app and a complementary Android app. As usual, what you can do depends which route you take to accessing your book library. For example: from the online web app (left picture below) you can "Make available offline" **(1)** any book that is in ePub format, whereas via the Android app (right picture below) you can Download **(2)** any book regardless of format.

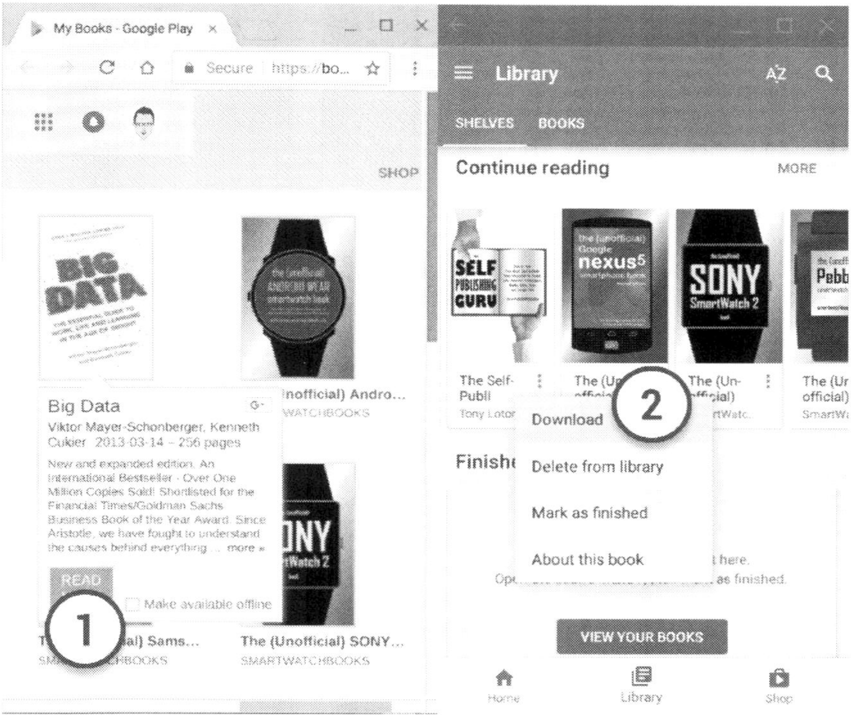

This following picture shows an e-book being displayed in the Chrome web browser, and you can see how it is possible to adjust the way that the content is displayed.

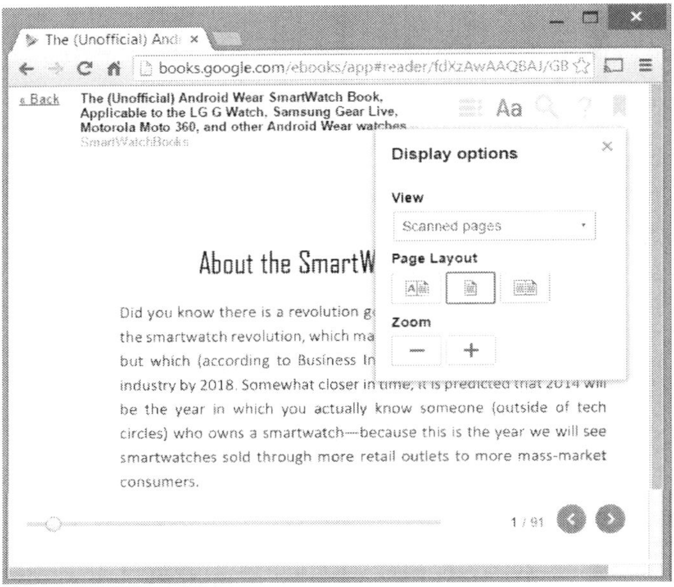

Not the Only Chromebook Bookstore

Google Play Books is not the only online bookstore and book-reading app that you can use with your chromebook or the Chrome browser. The other main contender is the Kindle Cloud Reader web app that allows you to access the Kindle bookstore and your existing Kindle library.

If you're starting your online book library from scratch with your chromebook and / or Android phone, you might standardize on Google Play Books. I also like the fact that Google Play books are usually available in PDF layout (which mirrors the printed book exactly) as well as in free-flowing ePub format.

If you already have an investment in Kindle books, you can still access those books while transitioning to Google Play Books... or not, if you prefer. But the fact is that both are equally accessible, so you really don't need to choose at all.

Google Payments

You can review the Google Play purchases you have made by visiting the Google Payments Centre at payments.google.com:

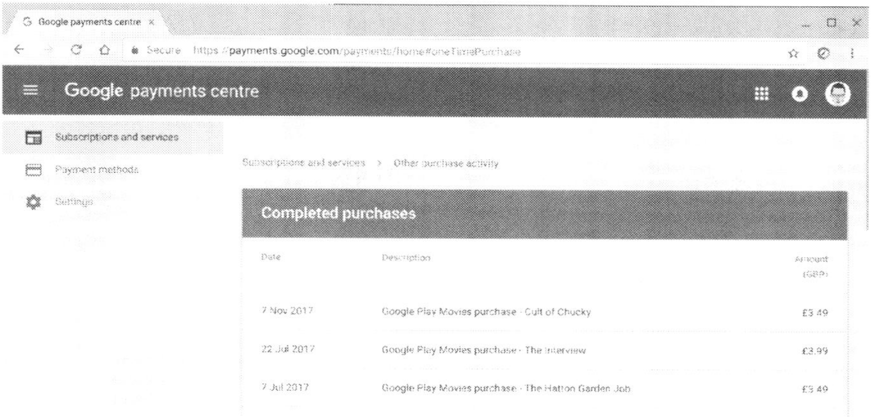

Chapter Summary

In this chapter I have presented the Google Play Store (which is home to media content) as distinct from the previously-described Chrome Web Store (which is home to Chrome web apps). Google Play allows you to preview, purchase or rent media such as movies, TV shows, music and books.

In the context of movies and TV shows, I told you how you can connect your chromebook to a "big screen" TV to watch those movies and TV shows in the style to which you have no doubt become accustomed, then I described the alternative Chromecast device for projecting such content (and even regular browser tabs) onto a big screen wirelessly.

In the context of Google Play Books, I explained that – while this may be the preferred option – you are at liberty instead to continue building your Kindle book library.

Cloud Computing Conundrums

The low-maintenance chromebook and the wider Google cloud computing paradigm present a set of conundrums in the form of tasks that you used to be able to perform quite easily using your traditional PC, but which the cloud computing approach makes more difficult. In this chapter I present some of those cloud computing conundrums, and (most helpfully) the potential solutions.

But first, let me begin by stating that from the very start the Chrome OS doesn't at all present one of the conundrums presented by the comparative Apple devices such as the iPad. Many of the financial trading web sites and other web sites that I used to use daily required my computing device (laptop, phone or tablet) to run Adobe Flash content in the web browser. On the iPad and on other Apple iOS-powered devices this was simply impossible, because those devices wouldn't run Flash at all. Chromebooks have no such limitation, and they run Flash web sites just fine, but I have to admit that this is becoming less important as many web are sites transitioning away from Adobe Flash and towards HTML5 for the presentation of dynamic content.

Okay, so much for what Chrome OS devices can do that the iPad can't. Now what about those things that chromebooks can't do?

Note that while some of this chapter is chromebook-specific, some of it is applicable to (but somewhat optional) when running the Chrome browser on your Windows PC. While you can use Google's Cloud Print and the Chrome Remote Desktop on a PC, you probably don't need to. But on a chromebook you pretty much have to.

Printing

The most obvious cloud computing problem is printing. Chromebooks were designed not to run locally-installed software, and this includes printer drivers, so there is little point trying to attach a printer directly to your chromebook computer via the USB port. If you try to do so, your chromebook should at least present a web page inviting you to "Add Classic printer or Add Cloud Ready" printer.

The conundrum of printing from a chromebook that does not allow printer drivers to be installed can be addressed in a number of ways as follows.

HP ePrint

Since the printing problem is not only a problem for users of chromebooks, but also a problem for users of smartphones and tablets that don't generally allow you to attach printers directly, a few years ago Hewlett Packard came up with an ingenious solution in the form of its ePrint range of printers.

These printers connect up to HP's ePrint service on the internet via your wireless router, and allow you to associate an email address with the printer. Printing on one of these printers from your chromebook, phone or tablet – even from miles away – can be as simple as sending your document as an email attachment to:

emailaddressofmyprinter@hpeprint.com (not a real email address)

Note that if the email address of your printer became widely known, anyone could print to it, although it's anyone's guess as to why they would want to.

If your chromebook is on the same wireless network as your HP ePrint printer, there is another way to print directly to the printer using the "HP Print for Chrome" app that is available in the Chrome Web Store. Once installed, you should henceforth be able to choose "Print" from Chrome **(1)**, change the print destination **(2)** to you HP Print for Chrome printer **(3)**, and then actually Print **(4)**:

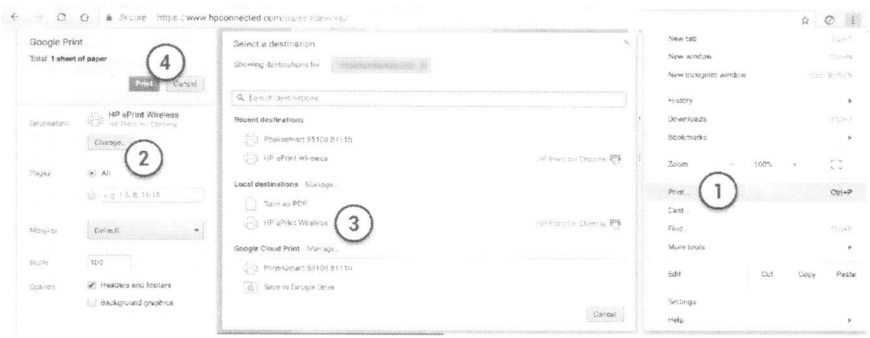

Note that in order to get my wireless HP printer to appear in the list of local destinations at all, I had to use the "Add printers by IP address" option in the HP Print for Chrome app, and to enter the IP address that my printer showed in its wireless settings.

Cloud Print

HP ePrint printers as well as many other kinds of printers can be registered with Google's Cloud Print facility that allows you to print from anywhere to any printer registered to your Google Account. Find instructions for connecting printers as cloud printers at:

https://www.google.com/cloudprint/learn/printers/

In simple terms, you can add a new printer by typing chrome://devices into the Chrome web browser to see which printers from your wireless network are available for connecting to Cloud Print. In this case, the HP Photosmart printer on my network has already been added:

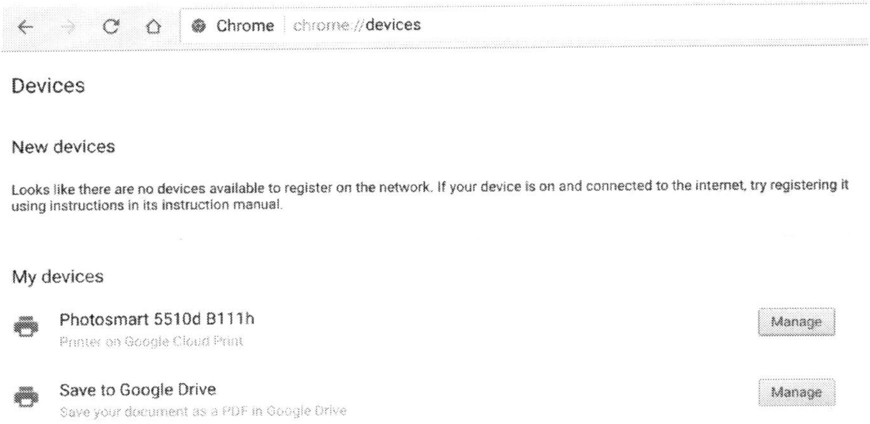

Once you've registered a printer with the Google Cloud Print service you can print to it as though the printer is attached to your chromebook. .

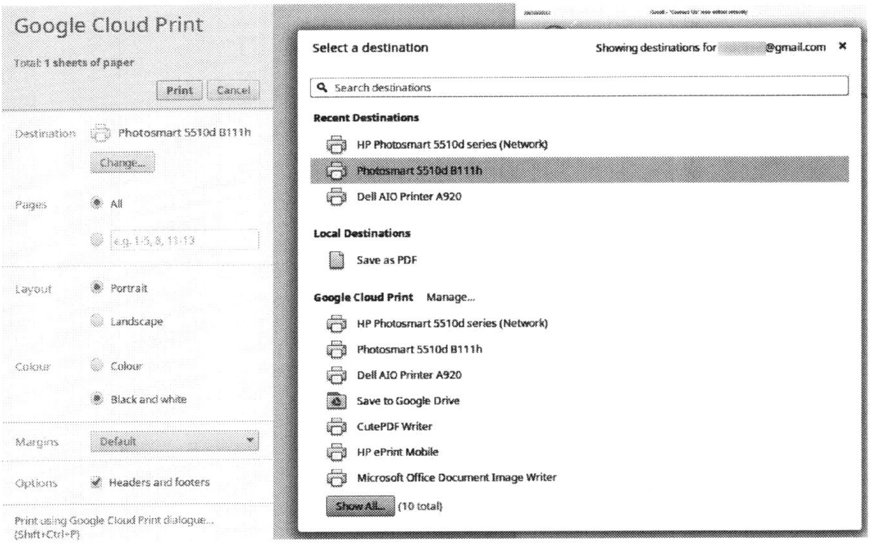

Note that alternatively you can "Save as PDF", which enables you to store a "printed" copy of your content (in this case an email message) as an electronic Portable Document Format (PDF) file in your chromebook's Downloads folder... from where you might copy it to your Google Drive for permanent safekeeping.

Cloud Print also allows you to see a list of print jobs and their print statuses:

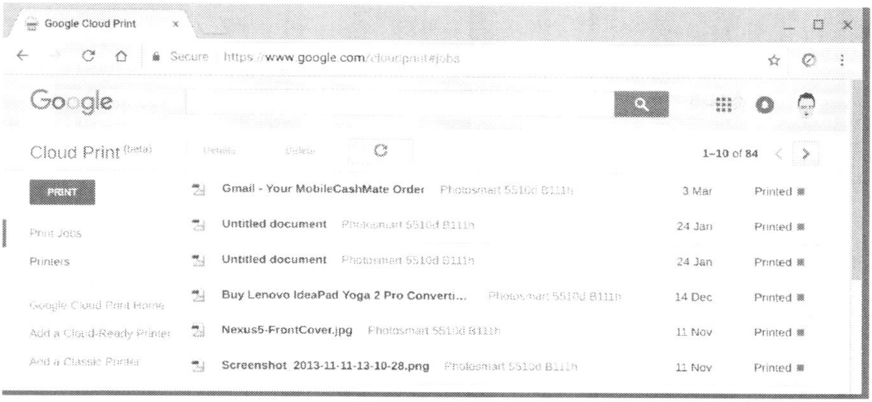

Connecting a PC Printer to Cloud Print

You can take advantage of any "classic printers" you have connected to a Windows PC by registering those attached printers to your Cloud Print account, so that they can be accessed remotely from your chromebook. Type chrome://devices into the Chrome browser on your PC, then click the "Add printers" button under the "Classic printers" heading to see something like this:

Once you have chosen which PC-attached printers to add to Cloud Print, you will see them as print destinations on your chromebook:

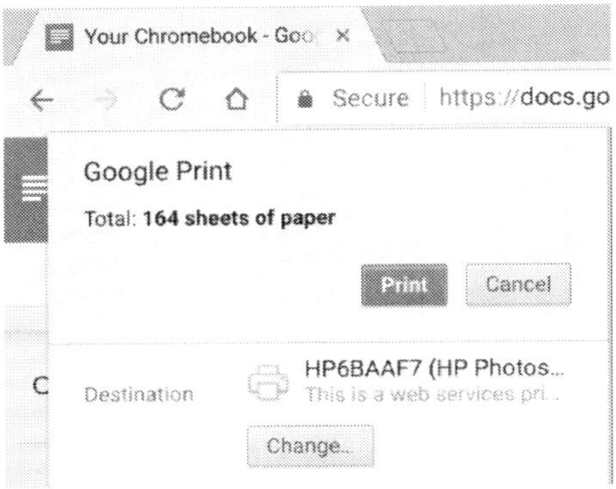

Accessing Windows Programs via the Chrome Remote Desktop

I reckon I can exist almost 100% *in the cloud*, simply interacting with Google Apps and the other websites I use on a regular basis. But as a book publisher I also used to do some pretty hardcore stuff using Microsoft Word.

Reconciling these two worlds – my desire to carry only a chromebook with me wherever I go, and my need to access the advanced features of Microsoft Word – presented me with a problem. Or did it?

I have a perfectly serviceable desktop PC that runs Microsoft Word, and I have a broadband router that allows this desktop PC to be always connected to the internet. If only there was a way to somehow "dial in" to this PC from my chromebook, and to interact with it via the chromebook keyboard and screen (from wherever I happen to be at the time), then I wouldn't be limited by the fact that I can't run Windows software directly on my chromebook.

You won't be surprised to learn that I'm leading up to the fact that... you can do exactly what I just described, by using the Chrome Remote Desktop. Here's how...

On Your PC

First you need to do a little setup at the PC end.

Using the Chrome web browser, visit the Web Store at chrome.google.com/webstore and search for "chrome remote desktop". Once located, install and launch the app. You will be prompted to select a Google Account with which to register the remote desktop, and you will be asked to authorize extended access to your computer.

The remote desktop has a "Remote Assistance" option which is intended for technical support staff to gain temporary access to someone else's computer, and a "My Computers" option that allows you to access and operate your home or office-based PC remotely from your chromebook.

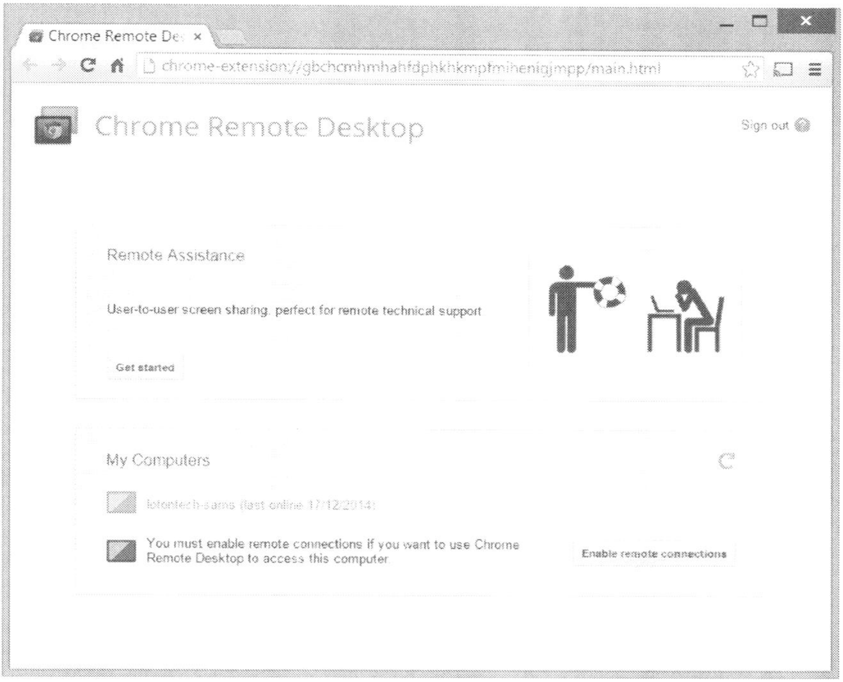

Upon clicking the "Enable remote connections" button shown in the previous screenshot, you will be prompted to enter a PIN that ensures only you can access your PC remotely. Once the remote desktop feature has been enabled, you should ensure that the PC (especially if a laptop) power settings are such that it will not go to sleep just when you really want to access it remotely.

On Your Chromebook

Once you've set up the PC end of the remote connection, you can launch the Chrome Remote Desktop app on your chromebook.

If you have to install the Chrome Remote Desktop app on your chromebook, make sure you install the web app version from the Chrome Web Store, not the equivalent Android app from the Google Play Store which (in my experience) doesn't work as well.

You should see your PC listed in the My Computers section of the page as shown below, and you can simply click (and enter your PIN) to connect.

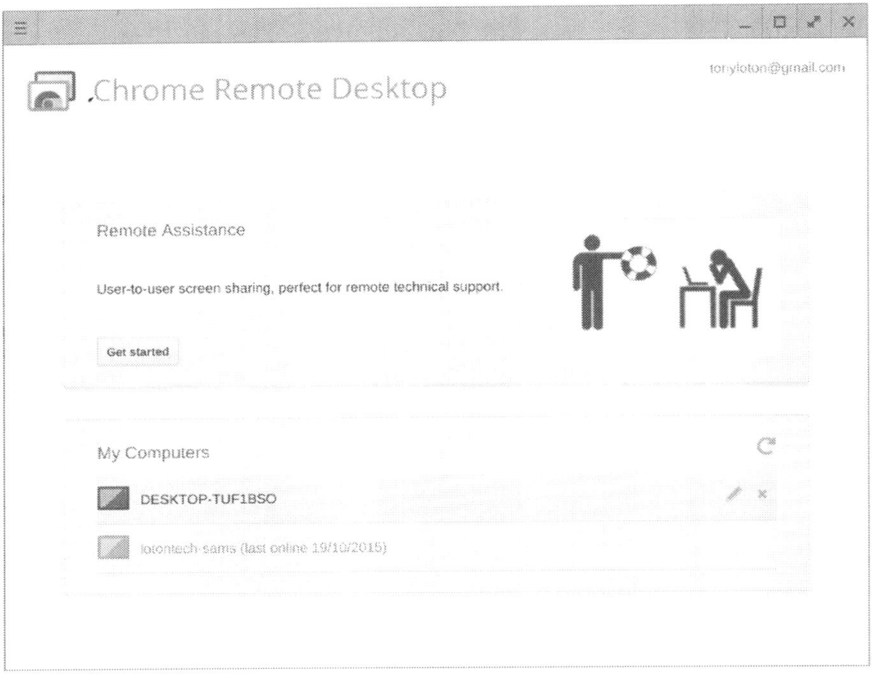

Everything you do on your PC screen will appear automatically on your chromebook screen, and vice versa:

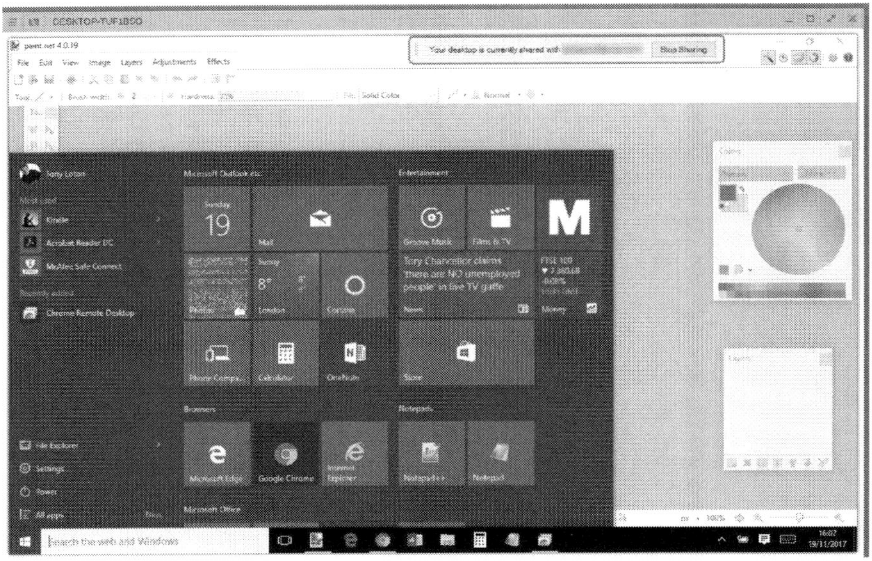

You can operate your PC from your chromebook as though the chromebook is your PC, and you can run all your favorite PC programs... even if you're in another room or another city. The previous picture shows my remotely connected Windows PC screen on display - and fully interactive - within a chromebook window.

Chapter Summary

The Chrome cloud computing model presents some interesting opportunities to work and play in ways that were simply not possible previously; but it also presents some challenges such as how to print and how to run the (Windows) software programs that you used to know and love. So in the chapter I have addressed some of those cloud computing conundrums. For many of you, this will have been the most useful chapter of the book.

When it comes to one of the solutions in particular - the Chrome Remote Desktop - I personally used to use this feature rather more than I expected; for example when sitting in my home study (chromebook on my lap) while the remotely-connected PC in my office some miles away.

Cloud Computing Without a Chromebook

Chromebooks may well be the perfect computers for cloud computing, but you don't actually need a chromebook at all in order to do your computing in the cloud. This chapter is for those of you who don't yet have a chromebook and would like to *try* Google's cloud computing services *before you buy* a dedicated chromebook computer. It is also for those of you who have bought (or are buying) a chromebook to use in addition to your existing Windows PC or Android smartphone or tablet, and you want all your devices to work well together.

This is one of the advantages of cloud computing—that you can access your cloud-stored documents and other files from any compatible device anywhere in the world.

Cloud Computing for Windows PC Users

To get a feel for how a chromebook works before you buy one, or to get a consistent experience when you switch between your chromebook and your Windows PC, you can simply launch the Chrome web browser on your PC and make sure everything you do is within the browser. Pretend it's the only program installed on your PC:

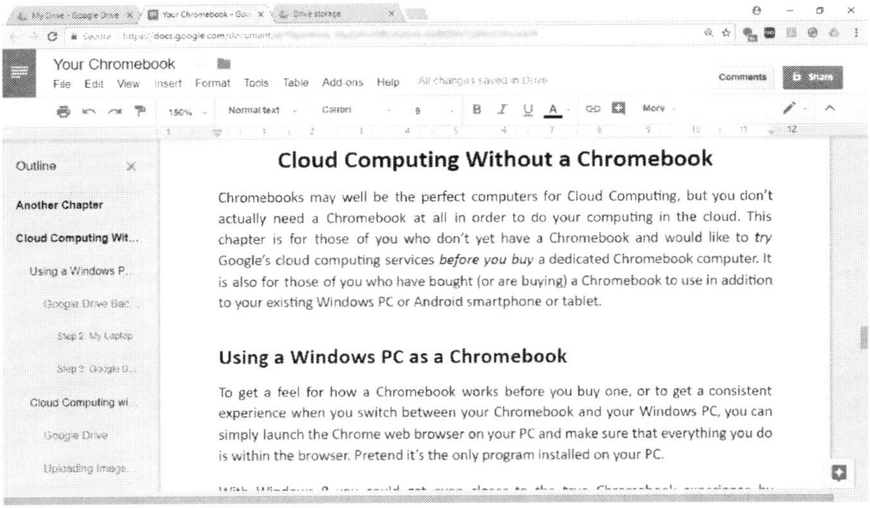

With Windows 8 you could get even closer to the true chromebook experience by launching Chrome in Windows 8 (Metro) mode so that it took over the whole screen and provided the same kind of App launcher (left) and notifications (bottom-right) as Chrome OS:

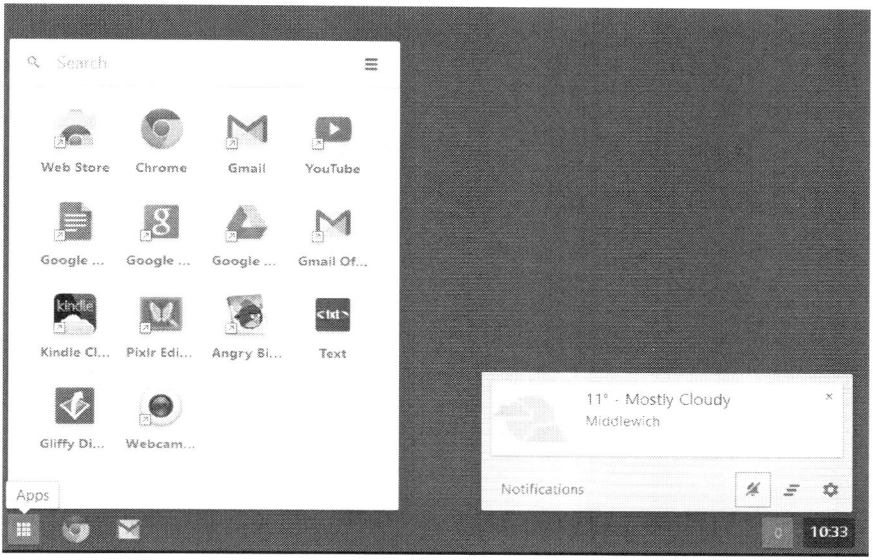

Don't get too excited about this since you can no longer do it, but my initial advice still stands about working wholly within the web browser to conjure up a chromebook-like experience on any other device.

Google Drive Backup and Sync

One of the benefits of cloud computing is to have your files backed-up automatically on the internet so that you no longer run the risk of losing them if your computer crashes. Along with this goes the ability to access your files using any compatible device from anywhere in the world. You can achieve both these aims by downloading the Backup and Sync program to your PC from www.google.com/drive/download/.

The setup follows a three-step process of signing in to your Google Account, choosing the PC folders to automatically backup to your Google Drive (first picture below), and deciding whether to sync the current contents of your Google Drive to your computer (second picture below).

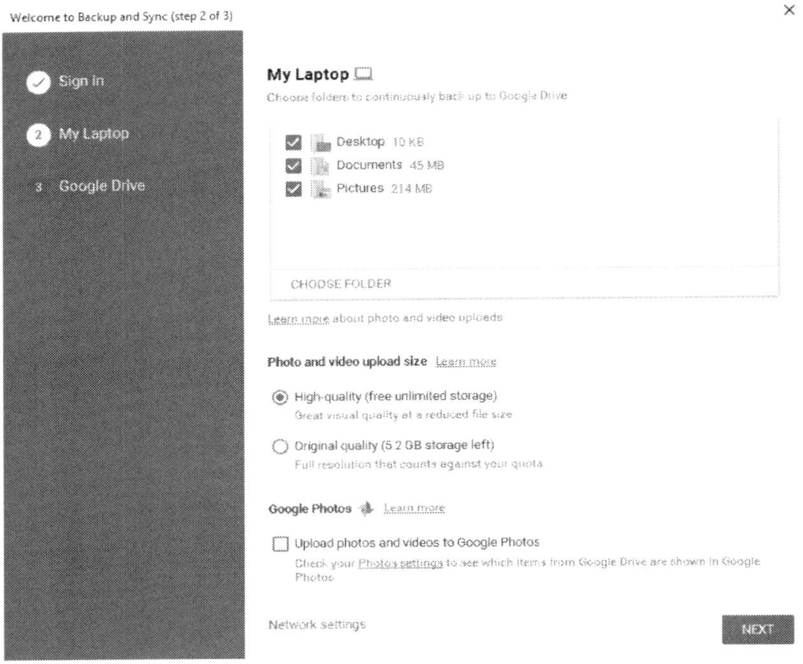

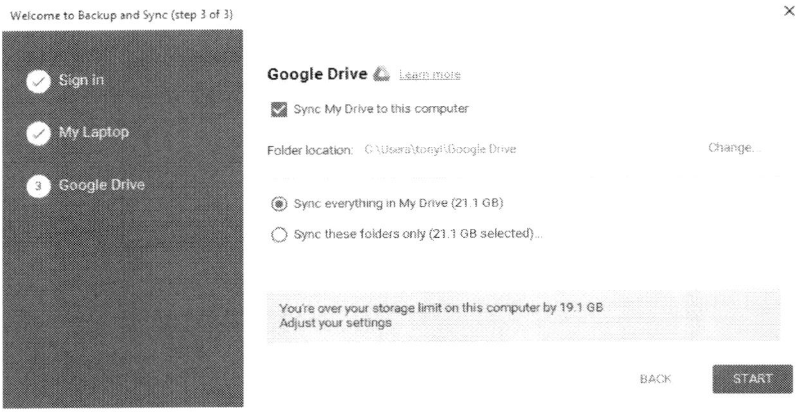

You will henceforth be able to see your chosen PC folders within the Computers section of your Google Drive at drive.google.com (see below), and the two sets of files will be kept perpetually in sync:

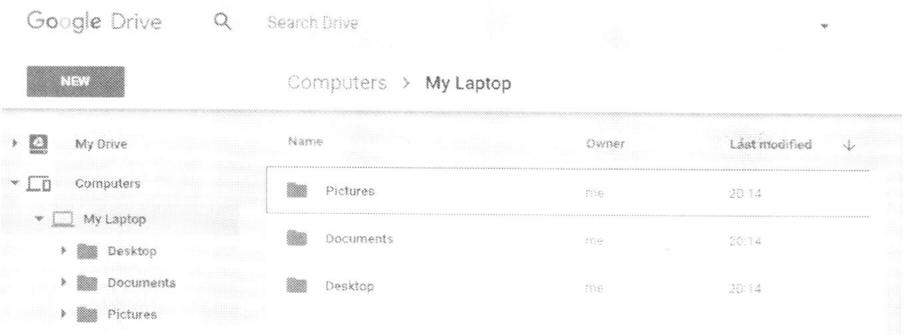

Cloud Computing for Android Users

Your Android smartphone or tablet can also act as a kind of chromebook if you confine all your activities to the Chrome web browser. Access the same Google Docs (at docs.google.com) and Google Drive (drive.google.com) that you can access from your chromebook or from your Windows PC running the Chrome web browser.

While it is perfectly possible to access your Google cloud files in this way, you will likely be prompted to use the dedicated Android apps for Google Docs and Google Drive (plus Google Slides) instead. You can install them from the Google Play Store.

Now that chromebooks are starting to support Android apps officially, using an Android tablet is a lot more like using a chromebook than it used to be; and vice-versa.

Google Drive for Other Devices

Google Drive is the gateway to your file storage area in the cloud; i.e. where your files are stored on Google's server computers. The Google Drive app for Android allows you to navigate your stored files and folders in much the same way that the File Explorer program allowed you to access the files and folders on your Windows PC. In the following picture you can see the Google Drive app for Android (leftmost), Google Drive displayed in the Android phone's Chrome web browser (middle), and Google Drive accessed via the traditional Microsoft Windows File Explorer (rightmost).

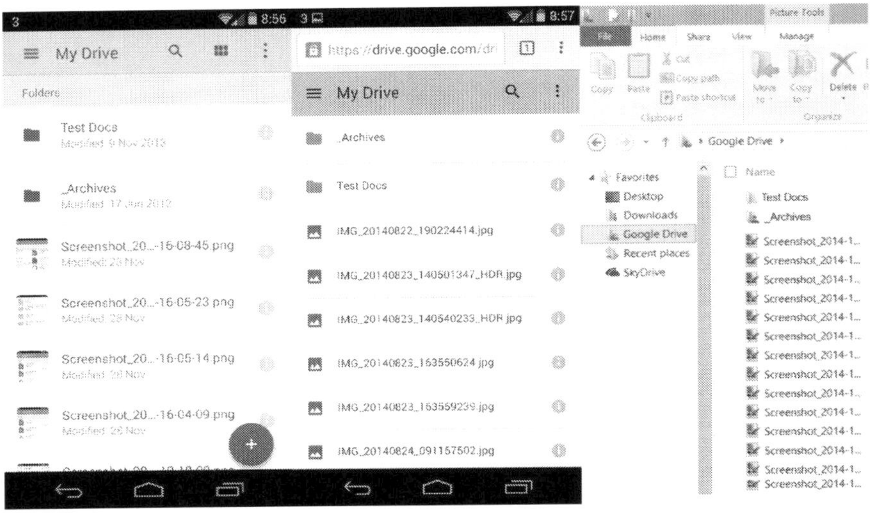

Thus there are several ways to access the exact same Google Drive files and folders from different devices.

Uploading Images and Other Files to Google Drive

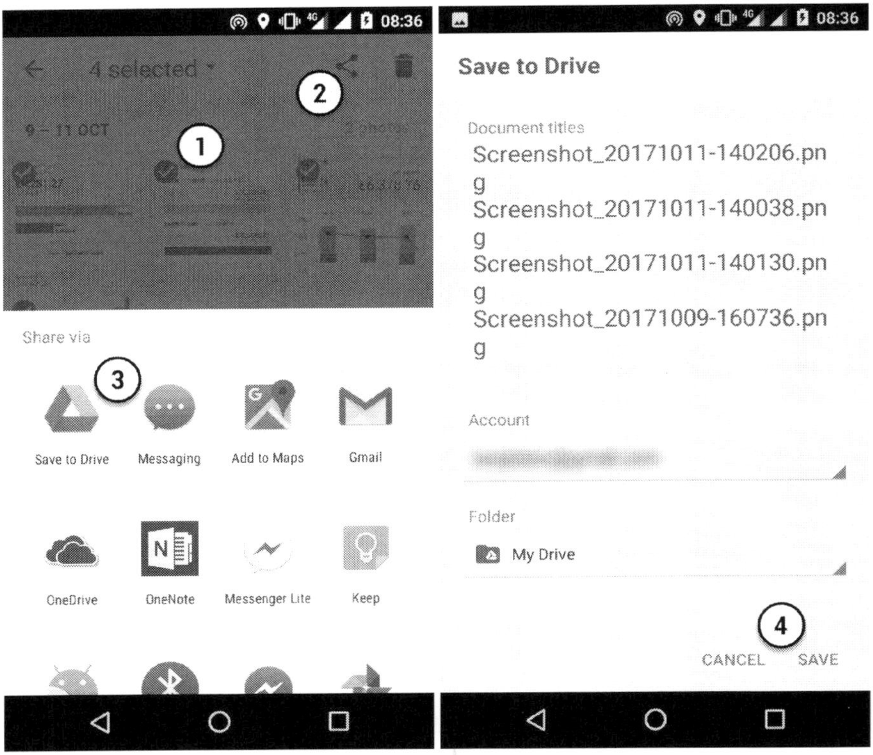

From the Android Gallery or Photos app you can multiple-select any photos or screenshots you have taken **(1 above)**, click the share icon **(2)**, and then "Save to Drive" **(3 and 4)**; but only if you have the Google Drive app installed on your phone.

It may not have escaped your notice that you could also upload the same photos, screenshots or other files to Microsoft's rival One Drive if you have the OneDrive app installed.

If you're using Google Photos, you will find that the photos which upload automatically from your Android phone are automatically made available from Google Drive.

Google Docs, Sheets and Slides Apps

You can think of Google Docs, Sheets and Slides as Google's equivalents of Microsoft Word, Excel and PowerPoint respectively. Although these apps are not exact equivalents of the Microsoft counterparts, they perform similar functions and have a degree of compatibility to the extent that you can import and export Microsoft file formats.

This is what those three apps look like in action on Android, and you might have to install them from the Google Play Store if they are not already installed on your Android device.

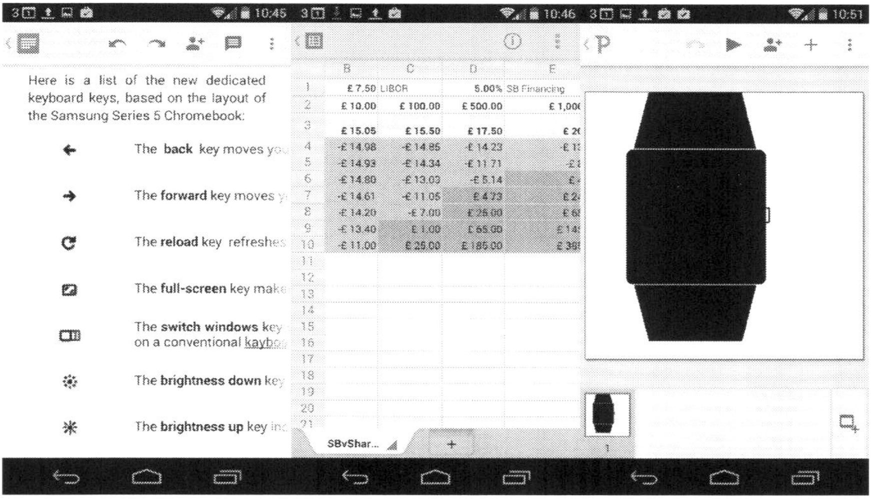

Not As Silly As It Sounds

Using an Android smartphone to create and edit Google documents, spreadsheets and presentations is not as silly as it sounds. Not only can this work well enough on the phone's touchscreen itself, and especially on an

Android tablet, but also it is possible – with a little ingenuity – to rig up an Android phone with a Bluetooth keyboard and mouse plus a big screen to simulate a desktop computer:

Google is Not the Only Cloud

Since this chapter has been about cloud computing without a chromebook, I should also say that it is possible to practice cloud computing without Google at all. Apple has its iCloud, Microsoft has the OneDrive (plus various other cloud services), and Amazon has its own set of cloud services and storage.

In general it makes sense to use the cloud solution provided by the company whose products you use most often: the OneDrive if you're a prolific user of Microsoft Office on a Microsoft Windows PC, iCloud if you have an iPhone or iPad, and the Amazon Cloud Drive if you have one of their devices or consume a lot of their content. That said—most of these cloud solutions can be accessed via a web browser on any device, and most of them have dedicated apps you can install on competitor devices. Just as you can install Google Drive on a

Windows PC, so can you install the Microsoft OneDrive app on an Android smartphone or access your OneDrive via the chromebook's web browser simply by visiting onedrive.com. I make this last point because in reality you will likely have multiple devices from multiple providers, and the whole point of cloud computing should be that you can access the same files from any device anywhere in the world.

Chapter Summary

In this chapter I have demonstrated how you can interact with Google's cloud computing services without a chromebook computer, either because you don't have one yet or because your chromebook is just one of the computing devices you use.

I concluded by telling you that there are equally-accessible cloud computing alternatives from Microsoft, Apple, Amazon, and many other companies that you may never have heard of.

Cloud Computing Case Study

It's all very well me telling you how you can now do almost everything via web apps in the cloud, but it's time for me to put my money where my mouth is by demonstrating how I can run my own business in the cloud... by creating and publishing the book you are reading now using only cloud-based tools accessed from my chromebook. Whereas in previous iterations I have been able to do most of my work "in the cloud" with some minor finishing touches using Windows programs, this time I really have worked entirely within the web browser on my chromebook to create this chromebook book. I promise.

Making the Manuscript

The first thing I need to do in my endeavor to publish a book is to actually write the manuscript for the book's content, which I have done in this case in the form of a Google Docs document. It's the one you're reading right now!

Page Setup

I intended to publish this book ultimately with a trim size of 5.5" x 8.5" (13.97cm x 21.59cm), which unfortunately is a size not supported by Google Docs, so I opted for the nearest size of "Statement (14 cm x 21.6cm)" which works well enough:

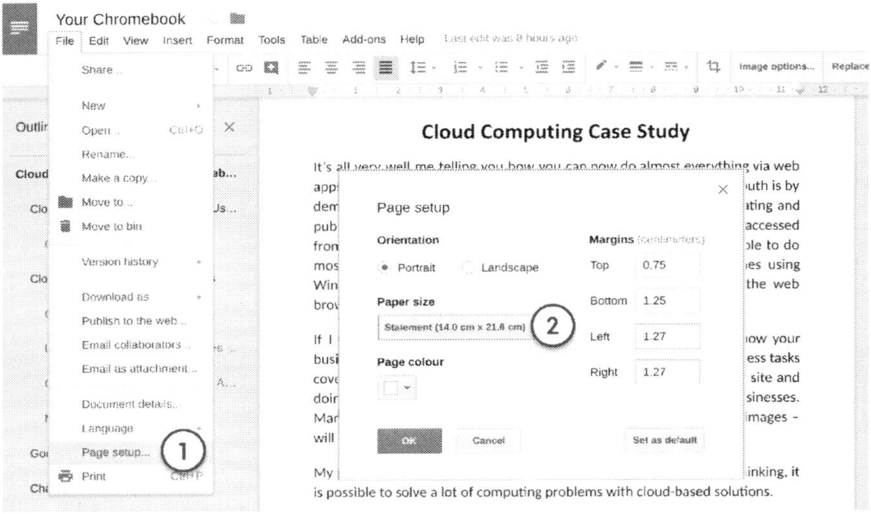

Note that the online edition of Microsoft Word allows you to specify a custom page size, which may be a better cloud-based choice is some circumstances.

Ideally a printed book would have an internal "gutter" of extra space on the inside edges of pages to allow for binding. This "mirror margins" feature is not supported by Google Docs or the Microsoft Word online edition at the time of writing, but I doubt you would even notice the slightly shifted pages in the printed book if I hadn't just told you about it! And for the Kindle edition of this book, it doesn't matter at all.

Styles

When writing any document using any word processor it is important to apply the built-in styles for "Normal" text and for headings such as "Heading 1" and "Heading 2". You can re-style these built-in styles by changing the font, font size, and characteristics (such as bold) and then right-clicking your selected text in order to access the context menu with the option (in this case) to "Update 'Heading 3' to match":

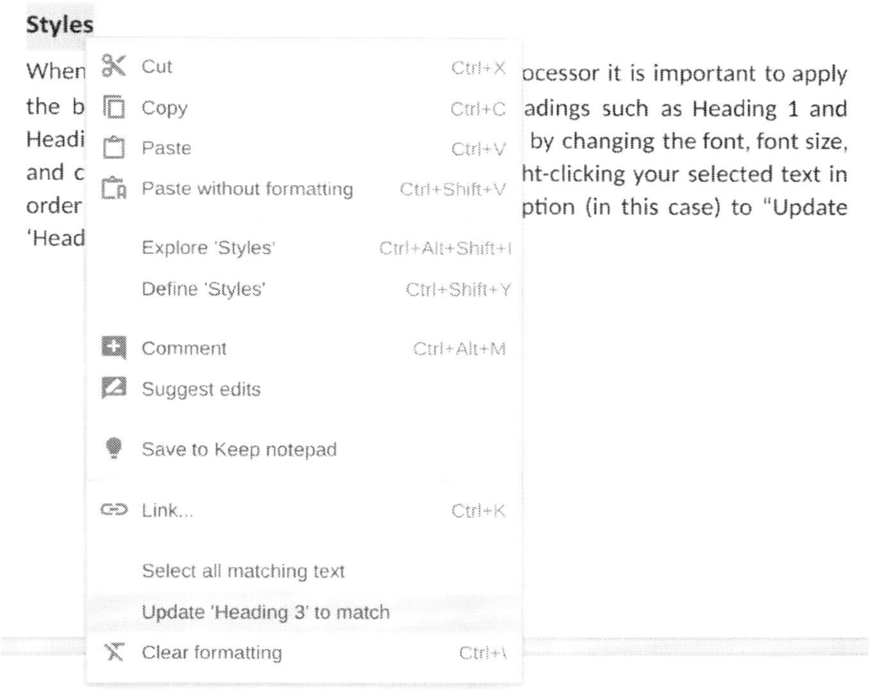

Headers and Footers

While it is perfectly possible to insert headers and footers onto the pages of a Google Docs document, it is not obvious (if at all possible) how to prevent those headers and footers from appearing on every single page. This is a problem when creating a printed book or report for which you do not wish the header to appear atop the title page or any new chapter page. In the absence of a per-section "first page header" feature, I have opted not to use headers but to use simple footers displaying merely the page number. This can be achieved simply by choosing one of the "Page number" options from the "Insert" menu.

Note that it is possible to have a different first page header and footer for the whole document, so that (for example) the title page of this book does not display the page number.

Images

This book contains many screenshots which I captured by pressing the **ctrl + switch windows** key combination on my chromebook. These get deposited by default in the Downloads folder, and I can open each one for cropping (using the local Files app) or more extensive editing (using the online Pixlr Editor) before inserting them into the manuscript via the Insert menu:

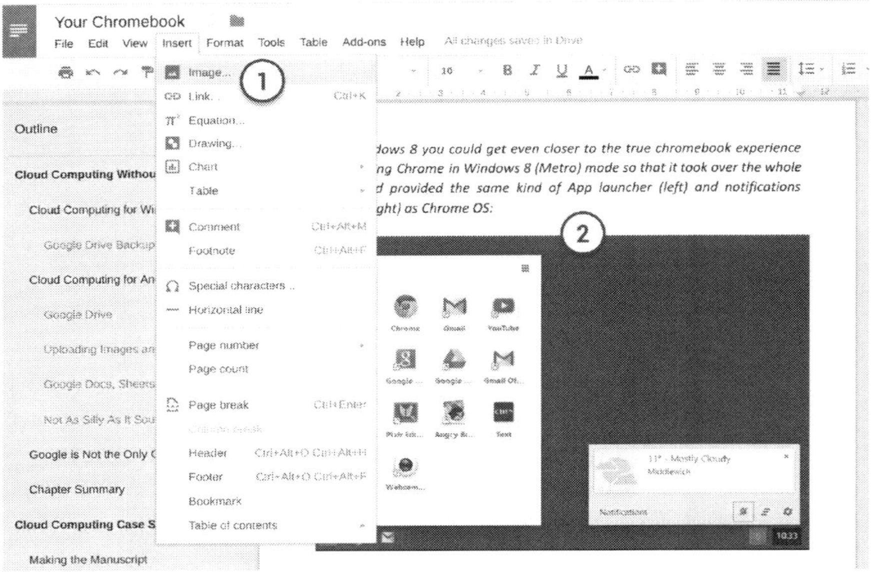

Table of Contents

Every book needs a table of contents, which is easy enough to insert within Google Docs. The inserted table of contents will work equally well for the Kindle edition (with hyperlinks) as it will for the print edition of the book (with numbers).

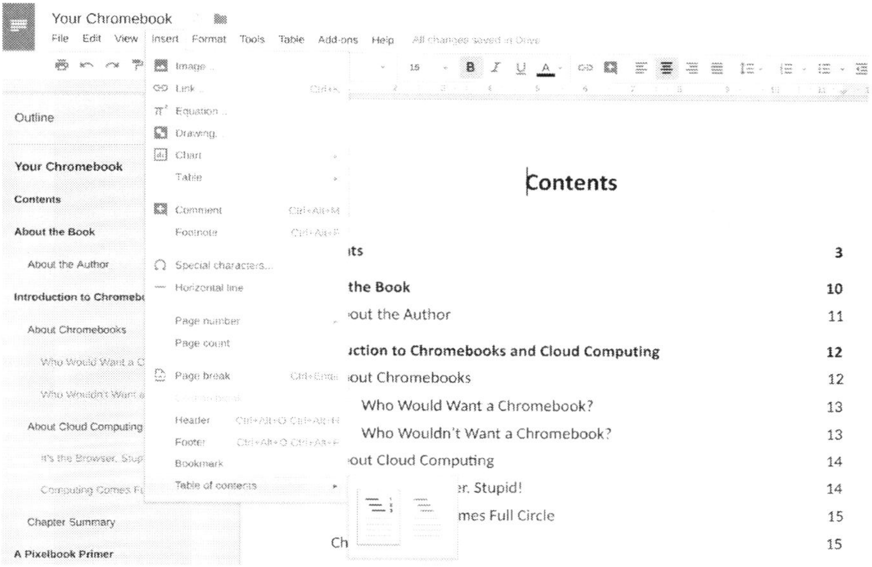

Peer Review and Editing

Every author should want their manuscript to be peer reviewed, edited, or simply proofread by someone else. I wanted my assistant to proofread this book, so I simply shared the Google Document with her by clicking the Share button and typing my invitation as shown next.

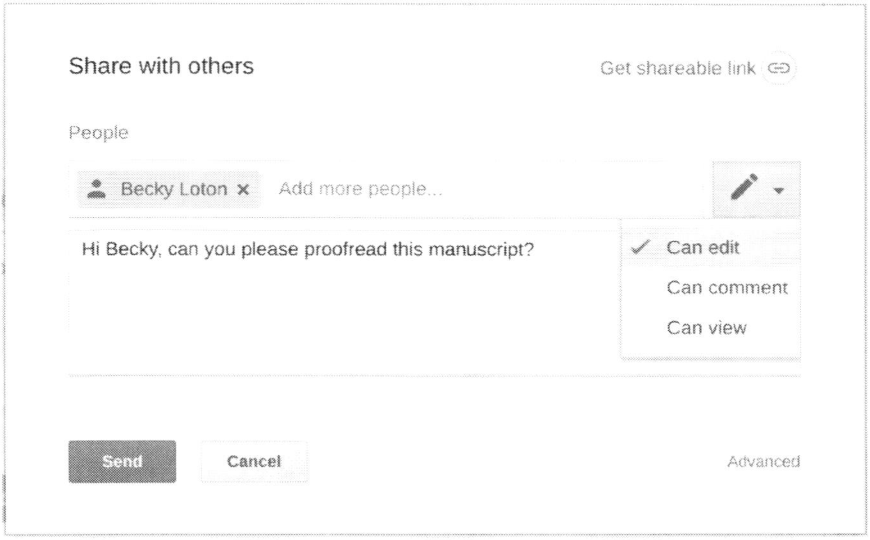

By specifying Becky as someone who "Can edit" the document, I am allowing her to insert comments and make textual changes directly in the document without us having to email copies of the manuscript back and forth.

Creating the Cover with Pixlr Editor

Every book needs a book cover, and creating the cover for my book could be done using the entirely web-based Pixlr Editor. You can think of this as a free web-based alternative to Adobe Photoshop, and one which does everything that my previous favorite PC-based paint program (PAINT.NET) does. I can set the size of the image to the exact trim size of the book, and crucially I can compose the content in layers so that (for example) the title text gets superimposed on the background picture underneath it. The end result can be saved in one of the popular image formats such as JPEG:

Now that many chromebooks support Android apps, there are many more possibilities for manipulating images with a chromebook, and there are additional online alternatives to the Pixlr Editor such as Sumo Paint.

Publishing as a Print Book via CreateSpace

This book was published in paperback format using Amazon's CreateSpace self-publishing platform at www.createspace.com. It's an entirely web-based publishing platform, and publishing via this route can be as simple as printing the Google Document as a PDF, downloading the Pixlr Editor cover image as a JPG, and uploading both to the CreateSpace publishing platform.

Downloading and Uploading the Book Interior

There are two ways to produce a PDF from a Google Docs document:

- **Download as | PDF Document (.pdf)** from the **File** menu.
- **Print** from the **File** menu, then **Save as PDF**:

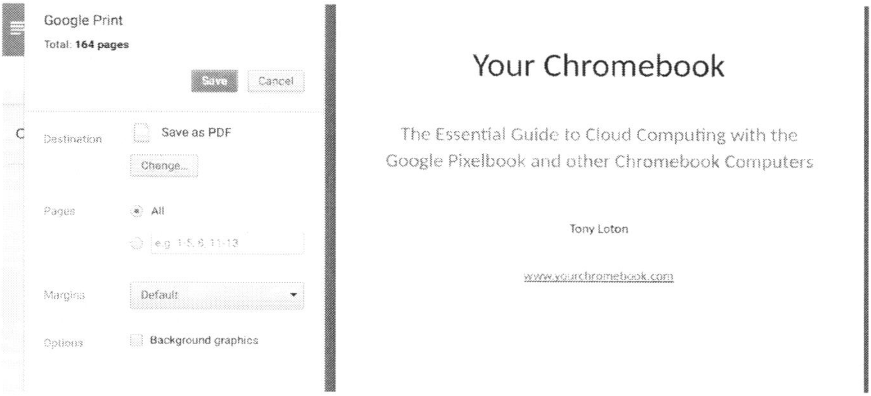

If you try the two approaches, you will see that the 'printed' PDF has a significantly bigger file size than the downloaded one, which is basically because it includes images at much higher quality. This is really important when it comes to producing a book in print, and it's why I prefer 'printing' the PDF from Google Docs rather than merely exporting it.

The upshot to all this is that when the PDF has been uploaded to the CreateSpace publishing platform from the chromebook's Downloads folder, the manuscript preview in CreateSpace looks like this:

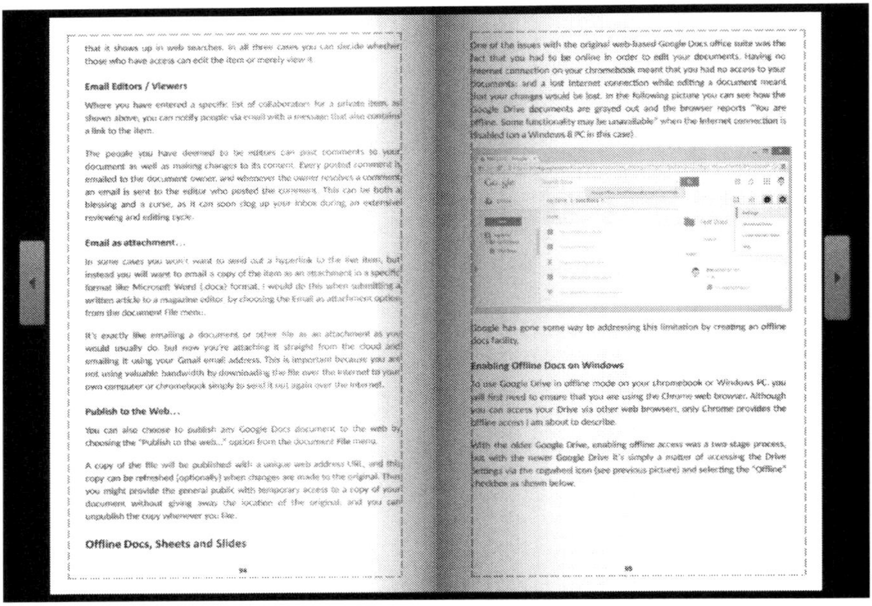

It's beginning to look a lot like a real book, isn't it?

Note that the CreateSpace publishing platform requires the Adobe Flash plugin that works perfectly well within the Chrome browser on a chromebook or Windows PC, but it's something you couldn't do using an iPad or other device that doesn't support Flash.

Downloading and Uploading the Book Cover

Just download two JPG images from Pixlr, one for the front cover and one for the back, and upload to the Createspace Cover Creator as shown next. It's as simple as that!

Well, it's not quite so simple, because JPEG can be a 'lossy' image format with details lost during compression. So be sure to have saved the Pixlr Editor image at 100% quality.

Publishing as a Kindle e-Book

This book was published in ebook form using Amazon's Kindle Direct Publishing (KDP) platform at kdp.amazon.com. It's entirely web-based, and publishing via this route can be as simple as downloading the Google Document in Microsoft Word (.docx) format, downloading the front cover Pixlr Editor image as a JPG, and uploading both to the KDP publishing platform.

The Book Web Site

Most published books have an associated web site to help sell the book or to provide additional information for readers. This book is no different, so I used GoDaddy to secure the yourchromebook.com domain name and then build the basic promotional page using their online website builder as shown next. I'm not telling you this to promote GoDaddy's services, but to demonstrate how it was possible for me to get a book website set up entirely online using nothing more than my web browser.

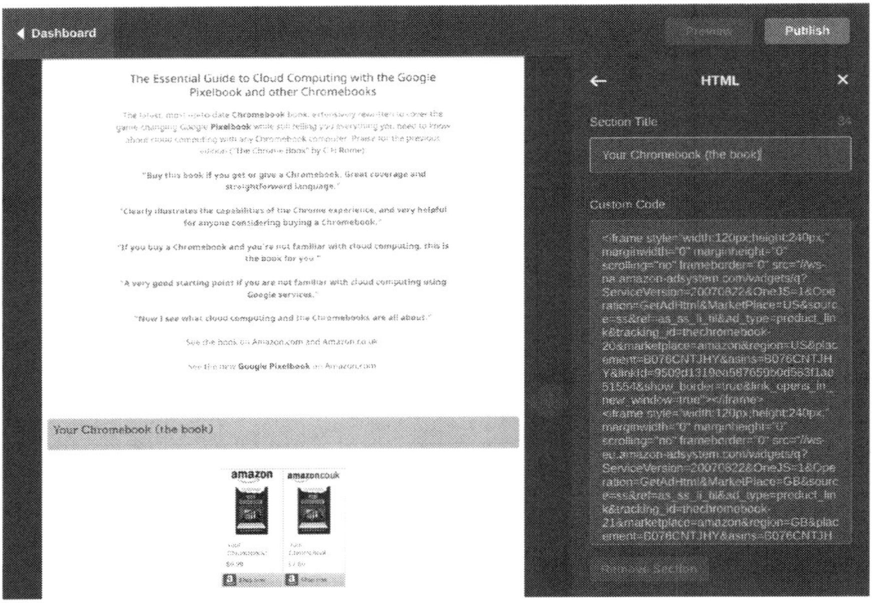

You may not be able to make out in this picture the Amazon sales links to my book, which I added using the online website builder's HTML feature. All I had to do was generate some affiliate links online using my Amazon Associates account (see below) and then paste the generated HTML code into the website builder's "Custom Code" box.

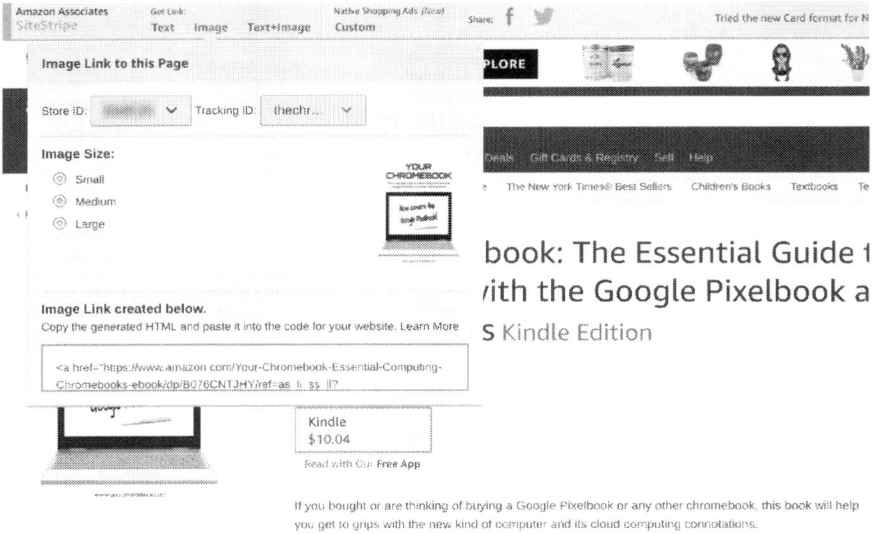

The ability to insert HTML into the website raises another interesting possibility. If I wanted to take book orders directly myself rather than directing potential purchasers to Amazon, I could generate the HTML code for a PayPal "Buy Now" button as shown next. Once again, entirely online.

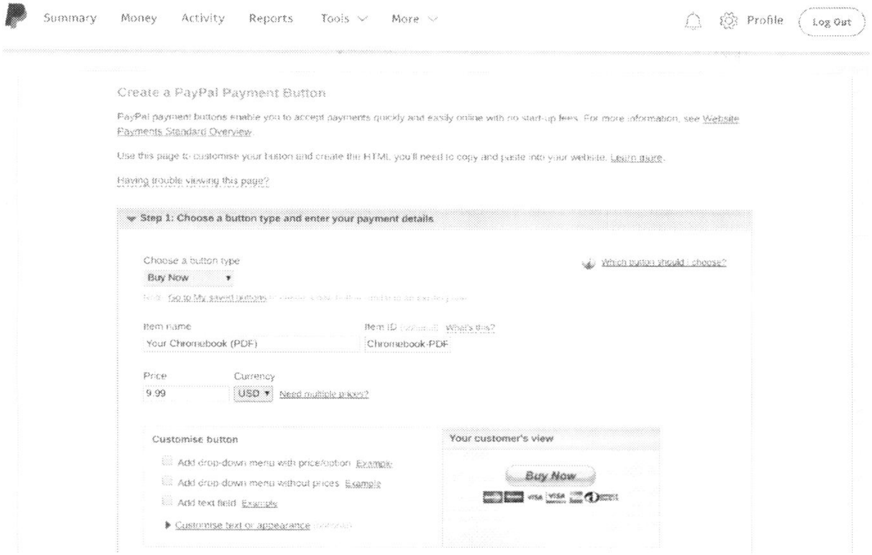

Before moving on to the next topic, I should mention that I need not have used the GoDaddy website builder to create my book-selling web site because Google allows us to create web pages in the cloud by visiting sites.google.com.

Doing the Accounts

Once you start selling products like books and e-books, you need to maintain a set of accounts that record your incomings and outgoings to be reported to the tax authorities. I used to use a Windows PC program called "Sage Accounts" to manage my company accounts, but now I use the fully web-based "QuickBooks Online" accounting package that can be found at qbo.intuit.com. Again, no PC required.

Yes, I know the amount of royalties I have included in this illustration may be wishful thinking!

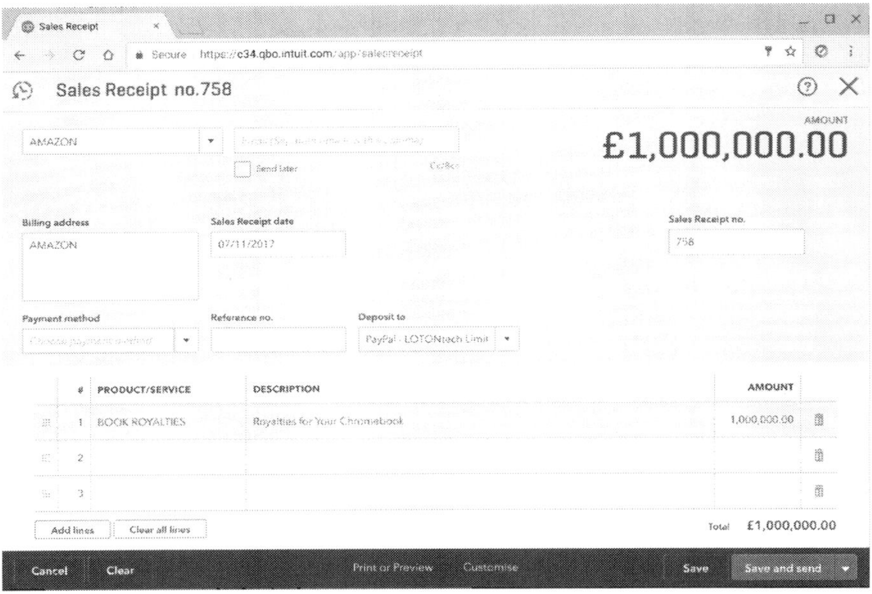

Chapter Summary

The aim of this case study chapter has not been to present you with a blow-by-blow account of exactly how to publish a book, how to set up a website, how to take online payments, and how to manage your business or personal accounts. The real aim has been somewhat more subtle: to demonstrate that all of these things are possible by utilizing web apps and other websites via your chromebook... no PC required (unless used merely to run the Chrome web browser). Cloud computing simply requires a little lateral thinking compared with what you may have been used to.

One negative reviewer (out of the many more positive ones) of a previous edition of this book commented along these lines:

*"I don't give a **** about the author's business. I want it to solve my problems."*

Well, that's a tricky one, because I can't possibly guess at every reader's problems. I can only build a case study around my own real-life experiences. So I hope you have taken this case study in the spirit it was meant: as an example of how a real-life person (me) can solve a set of real-life problems (specifically my business problems) by cloud computing with Chrome; with a view to hinting at possible similar solutions to *your* computing problems.

If I can run my business in the cloud, then maybe so can you. I know your business is unlikely to be a publishing business, but many of the business tasks covered by this case study - like creating documents, creating a web site and doing some basic e-commerce - will be applicable to many different businesses. Many of the technical tasks - like word processing and manipulating images - will be applicable to many business and personal computing scenarios. With a little ingenuity and lateral thinking, it is possible to solve a lot of computing problems with cloud-based solutions.

For Advanced Users Only

"Beware all ye who enter here!"

Was that sufficient warning? Good, because in this chapter I present some of the more advanced things you might do with your chromebook

Running Linux Programs (including Skype) on a Chromebook

First, a confession:

Apart from a lttle bit of editing, I've not updated the following information for this edition of the book, simply because I no longer have any need to extend the functionality of my Pixelbook chromebook by installing the Linux operating system side-by-side with Chrome OS. The combination of web apps complemented by Android apps is sufficient for my needs.

The Chrome OS operating system serves pretty much all the needs that we "cloud computing converts" might have, albeit via some roundabout routes at times. But since the Chrome OS sits atop the Linux operating system core, many of the more advanced chromebook users may speculate about whether their chromebooks can actually run the full-scale Linux operating system as an alternative to (or as well as) the Chrome OS. When first formulating this guidance for early chromebooks, it was a reasonable question because Linux provided the only route to running some native programs (such as Skype) that were not supported by the browser-based Chrome OS.

There are several ways to achieve the feat of running Linux on a chromebook, but the most effective and flexible way was - and for all I know, still is - by using a utility program called Crouton. So now let's look at how to "soup up your chromebook with Crouton" (get the joke?).

Soup Up Your Chromebook with Crouton

This sequence of steps may differ slightly for different models of chromebook, and some chromebook models may require you to throw a physical switch in order to enable the developer mode. For the record, these steps were performed on a Chromebook Pixel.

Note also that enabling the developer mode in the first step will cause the chromebook's local storage to be wiped, but this need not be a problem because all of your important data files should be stored safely on your Google Drive. It's best for me to forewarn you, though.

Step #1: Enable Developer Mode

1. Shutdown your machine.
2. Press and hold **esc + refresh** while pushing the power button to switch on your computer.
3. Press **ctrl + d** to be prompted to enable developer mode, followed by enter.
4. The machine will take some time to reboot, but you can speed up the reboot by pressing **ctrl + d** again.

Step #2: Install Crouton

1. Download Crouton from http://goo.gl/fd3zc.
2. Press **ctrl + alt + t** to launch a terminal window and type shell followed by the **enter** key.
3. Now type **sudo sh -e ~/Downloads/crouton -t xfce,touch** (followed by **enter**) to install Crouton.
4. Follow any prompts during the installation, and then finally...
5. Type **Done!** Start up an XFCE session with **sudo startxfce4** to start a Linux XFCE desktop session.

Unlike in an operating system dual-boot scenario, Crouton allows you to switch freely between the Linux and Chrome OS desktops using the following key combinations:

- On ARM processor chromebooks (e.g. the original Samsung) use the **ctrl + alt + shift + back** and **ctrl + alt + shift + forward** key combinations.
- On Intel processor chromebooks (e.g. Acer or Chromebook Pixel) use the **ctrl + alt + back** and **ctrl + alt + forward** (followed by **ctrl + alt + refresh**) key combinations.

The following picture shows the Linux desktop on my Chromebook Pixel after I made some changes to increase the screen font size etc. in the Linux display settings, without which the text would be microscopically small on my chromebook Pixel's super hi-res screen.

Note how on this Linux desktop I am running Skype, which at the time of writing (a few years ago) could otherwise not be run on a chromebook. Also notice the file manager window via which I am saving the captured screenshot into the Linux file system's Downloads folder; thereby allowing me to clarify that that this is the very same Downloads folder as the one presented by the Chrome OS in the Files app.

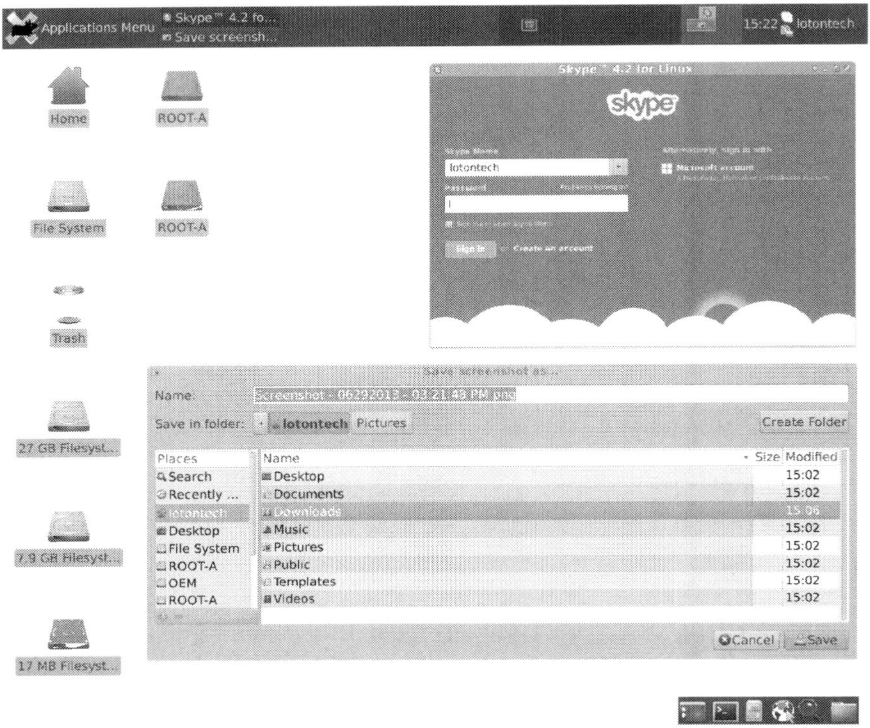

Getting Back to Normal

If, like me, you're actually not that keen on using the chromebook's developer mode in order to run Linux alongside the Chrome OS, you will be pleased to know that you can get "back to normal" simply by rebooting your chromebook and pressing the **spacebar** followed by the **enter** key on the boot screen to disable the developer mode. All local data will be wiped, and your chromebook will return to normal.

The ChrUbuntu Alternative

While Crouton offers the most flexible way of running Linux in addition to the Chrome OS on a chromebook, it's not the only way. For those advanced users who prefer a more traditional "dual boot" scenario in which you choose your operating system at startup, there was - and most likely still is - an alternative tool called ChrUbuntu. Google it if you're interested.

Updating Your Chromebook Over a Mobile Connection

From time to time you will need to update your chromebook with the latest system software., which may be easier said than done if you find that the required download won't commence while you're on a mobile network.

Personally, I've not needed to do this even though I rely wholly on the mobile data connection provided by my tethered Android phone, but this may be because it acts as an ordinary Wi-Fi hotspot. Should you find yourself in the sorry situation of not being able to update your chromebook while not connected to fixed broadband over Wi-Fi, I found the following steps online:

- Press the **ctrl + alt + t** key combination to open a terminal window.
- Type **update_over_cellular enable**.

Close the terminal window, ignore the warning, and... Hey Presto!

Resetting and Recovering Your Chromebook

Chromebooks and the installed Chrome OS are intended to be pretty robust and not as crash-prone as earlier Windows PCs. Nonetheless, there may come a time when you need to reformat your chromebook back to its factory state, or recover it completely. Particularly if you have attempted some of the more advanced ideas (like co-installing Linux) described in this chapter.

Powerwash

From the Advanced section of the chromeboook Settings at chrome://settings you can Powerwash the device in order to take it back to its original factory state. This can be useful to "wipe the slate clean" when you sell or give away your chromebook to someone else.

This is irreversible, and any files stored locally on your chromebook will be lost forever, so think carefully before performing this operation. On the other hand, with all of your important files stored safely in the cloud, you have less to worry about than you did when resetting a traditional PC to its factory state.

The Chromebook Recovery Utility

If your chromebook is not operating correctly, and a Powerwash doesn't fix it, you will need to use another chromebook (only some models supported), or a PC or Mac to create recovery media on a USB drive or SD card. Locate the "Chromebook Recovery Utility" in the Chrome Web Store, install and run it to create a recovery media USB drive or SD card that you can then insert into your originally chromebook.

Your inoperable chromebook should be showing a "Chrome OS is Missing or Damaged" screen, which will begin the recovery process as soon as you insert your valid recovery media into the device.

Chapter Summary

In this chapter I described how you might extend the functionality of your chromebook by co-installing the Linux desktop operating system, though I no longer do so myself.

I also told you how you can reset (by power-washing) and recover your chromebook if things go wrong.

Our Heads in the Clouds

You probably found that, like me, you were already spending 90% of your computing time on the web without even realizing it: reading and responding to emails, reading the news, and doing your online banking. You didn't need an over-engineered and virus-prone PC plus expensive software to do those things.

It may be true that you really do need to run some Windows PC software from time to time, but it doesn't mean you have to carry a PC around with you, especially if it's a desktop! Leave it at home or in the office, and connect to it remotely using the Chrome Remote Desktop app. It should work from any chromebook model; but on the supersize screen of the Chromebook Pixel or Google Pixelbook I have found it to be just like sitting right in front of the PC screen. Otherwise, you might think about meeting your non-cloud-computing needs by souping up your chromebook with Crouton (Linux).

The previous comment notwithstanding, I have made it clear throughout that I actually like the idea of going 100% cloud. What finally prompted me to aim towards full time residence in the cloud was the fact that, a few years ago, the screen on my Windows laptop computer flickered and died thereby rendering it my new 'desktop' computer with an external TV screen plugged in. It wasn't much use to me on the road, and in the time taken to consider a repair or replacement I became ever-more-reliant on whichever of my family's or friends' computers or other web-connected devices came to hand. However and wherever I logged in, I had almost instantaneous access to the important documents I was working on via Google Drive. There was no need to worry about a catastrophic hard disk crash, or whether I had remembered to backup my data yesterday.

Fast forward to 2017, and I find myself sitting on my bed writing these very words in a Google Docs document using my Google Pixelbook (but it could be any other chromebook). With one tap of the chromebook "switch windows" key I can check my Gmail in the Chrome browser, and in a separate browser tab I can update an entry in my Google Calendar. Meanwhile I am listening to a song playing in the background via the chromebook's built-in audio player.

In previous editions of this book I summarized how I had transitioned almost entirely to cloud computing, but not actually entirely. The fact was that there were some things I needed to do in my personal and business lives that were simply not possible without a Windows PC. However, in the course of rewriting the case study chapter, I discovered that I can now do everything that I need to do using nothing but my chromebook. And I have every incentive to do so, literally, because of the whopping £1000+ "investment" I have made in the top-of-the-range 2017-vintage Google Pixelbook compared with my more modest original investment of £229 in the October 2012-vintage Samsung Chromebook. After committing to such an investment, I wanted to make this cloud computing thing work for me... and I does.

The question is—will it work for you?

Google is Not the Only Cloud

While I have focused on cloud computing with Google hardware, software and services, I have assumed - or at least suggested - that you will adopt the set of cloud computing solutions offered by Google: Gmail for your email, Google Docs (via Google Drive) as your office application suite, and so on. But Google is not the only cloud computing show in town.

Those of you with a Microsoft Live ID or Outlook email address can create and store Microsoft Word, PowerPoint, and Excel documents on your OneDrive at onedrive.live.com. You might have so much investment in Microsoft Outlook as your email provider that you're not quite ready to switch to Gmail just yet.

The good news is that the Chrome browser is simply a web browser, so - even when running on a dedicated chromebook computer - it should allow you to use alternative cloud solutions as well as (or instead of) those provided by Google. Indeed, Google is more open than some providers to the prospect of you using the best third-party solutions for your needs, else why would they provide a Chrome Web Store populated with third-party solutions?

Having painted this rosy picture of every vendor coexisting in the cloud in peace and harmony, I should warn you that you will need to double-check that your alternative cloud computing suite really will run on your chromebook + Chrome combo. Some Microsoft web sites used to require or at least encourage you to install their Windows-dependent Silverlight browser extension, but this now seems not to be the case so much.

Even if your alternative cloud computing suites run faultlessly, you may need to think about how the various cloud computing solutions fit together:

- Want to reroute your incoming email messages from Hotmail or Yahoo! Mail to your Gmail Inbox, or reroute your incoming Gmail to one of the other providers? No problem at all.
- Want to write a document initially using Google Docs, and then download it in Microsoft Word (.docx) format for uploading to your Windows OneDrive for further editing? No Problem.

- Want to go the other way, and export a document created with the Microsoft Word Web App in a format other than the default .docx format? Well, it may not be so easy because the Microsoft Office Web Apps are designed to be an adjunct to the fully paid-up Microsoft Office Suite—so they assume that you have Word installed locally on your PC even though you are using the web-based alternative.

In a nutshell, interoperability between cloud computing solutions should be possible, and as my case study showed—with a little ingenuity and lateral thinking...it is. But, I have found that I can save myself a great deal of time and effort by wherever possible making Google my "one stop shop" for cloud computing solutions.

When it comes to accessing my Google cloud, I don't have to do so from a Google device such as a chromebook, even though I prefer to. I can access my Gmail and Google Docs from an Android mobile phone or tablet (okay, these are Google devices) or from a traditional Windows PC running the Chrome browser.

The choices are yours to make; but when all's said and done, for me, it's Google all the way.

The Future of Cloud Computing

Cloud computing with Chrome currently means accessing web sites or installing web apps that have been built using HTML (now HTML5). The construction of the web pages is handled server-side, but the action - and crucially the interaction - takes place within the browser.

In the case of the Chrome Remote Desktop things are rather different, with the browser acting merely as a screen to display whatever video content is transmitted from a remote computer. This is also the case...

...in professional IT environments where technologies such as Citrix are used to present a moving image of software running on a remote computer.

...with the Microsoft Azure program that allows programs to be deployed into remote Microsoft datacenters and streamed to local computers.

...for game streaming services that store and execute the games on a central server computer while streaming the games' video to (and capturing user interaction from) a local computer.

In this cloud computing model the client computer or web browser simply needs to be able to display streamed video content and relay user actions back to the central servers. This true thin-client computing has only really become viable with the ubiquity of high-speed broadband internet connections that reduce latency (i.e. network delay) to a minimum. But it arguably holds the key to the future of cloud computing—a future in which hardware and software compatibility is a thing of the past; a future in which you really will be able to run any program from any device anywhere in the world as easily as tuning into your favorite TV channel.

How Did I Help You?

Hopefully you found this book informative and enjoyable, in which case I encourage you to take the time to leave a positive review on Amazon.com, Amazon.co.uk, Google Play, or wherever you bought this book.

I look forward to reading your kind and constructive comments, and you might also like to visit this book's web site at www.yourchromebook.com.

26262092R00085

Printed in Great Britain
by Amazon